Sinatra: Up and Running

Alan Harris and Konstantin Haase

Beijing · Cambridge · Farnham · Köln · Sebastopol · Tokyo

Sinatra: Up and Running
by Alan Harris and Konstantin Haase

Copyright © 2012 Alan Harris. All rights reserved.
Printed in the United States of America.

Published by O'Reilly Media, Inc., 1005 Gravenstein Highway North, Sebastopol, CA 95472.

O'Reilly books may be purchased for educational, business, or sales promotional use. Online editions are also available for most titles (*http://my.safaribooksonline.com*). For more information, contact our corporate/institutional sales department: (800) 998-9938 or *corporate@oreilly.com*.

Editors: Simon St. Laurent and Mike Hendrickson   **Cover Designer:** Karen Montgomery
Production Editor: Melanie Yarbrough   **Interior Designer:** David Futato
Proofreader: Melanie Yarbrough   **Illustrator:** Robert Romano

Revision History for the First Edition:
  2011-11-21 First Release
See *http://oreilly.com/catalog/errata.csp?isbn=9781449304232* for release details.

ISBN: 978-1-449-30423-2

[LSI]

1321888247

Table of Contents

Preface

When people speak of Ruby web development, it has historically been in reference to the opinionated juggernaut that is Rails. This is certainly not an unfounded association; Hulu, Yellow Pages, Twitter, and countless others have relied on Rails to power their (often massive) web presences, and Rails facilitates that process with zeal.

Why, then, are people so interested in Sinatra, the tiny little domain-specific language that could?

Rails was a breath of fresh air to many developers exhausted by the "old ways"; Sinatra enters the arena with a similar game-changer: a beautifully minimalistic, "I'll get out of your way" approach. No generators, no complex folder hierarchies, and a brief yet expressive syntax that maps closely to the functionality exposed by the Hypertext Transfer Protocol verbs.

In short, Sinatra is for classy web development.

Our goal is to provide the core concepts and accompanying examples to help you feel comfortable using Sinatra as quickly as possible. By the end, you should have a working knowledge of Sinatra and how it fits into the larger Ruby web development ecosystem. You should know when Sinatra will get the job done quickly and when it might be better to lean on Rails, Padrino, or similar frameworks. You should also have a better sense of the internals of Sinatra, as well as the Rack specification and accompanying gem.

 No worries, we won't short-change you on the reference aspects; you can certainly return to this book to recall how to perform daily tasks without excessive searching.

With that said, let's get you up and running.

Who This Book Is For

Sinatra: Up and Running is for developers with some Ruby experience under their belt, and ideally some web development experience as well. Some concepts that are core to web development (the HTTP specification, HTML, CSS, etc.) are critical to understanding how to be productive with Sinatra; we recommend that you have at least a passing familiarity with these concepts to make the experience a little easier.

If you've written some web applications before but not specifically in Ruby, that's no problem. Our discussion of other tools is primarily limited to comparing and contrasting with how Sinatra does things.

Our plan is to try to address the needs of several distinct camps of readers: those with a Ruby web development background in Rails but no experience with Sinatra, as well those who are familiar with Sinatra but would like a tour of its internals and philosophy. Where possible, we'd also like to help bring developers without direct web experience into the fold. Pretty tricky if you think about it, but we'll do our best to speak to all the seats in the house by the conclusion.

Given these stated goals, we've divided the materials into three sections. The beginning of the book focuses on the bare minimum you need to know to work with Sinatra. Here you'll find the fundamentals, such as how to craft routes, manage sessions, create views, and so on. Immediately afterward, we will lift the veil and examine some of the techniques behind the scenes, which will open up a world of possibilities for implementation and integration. Finally, we will wrap up the discussion with some practical applications, including developing a GitHub-powered blog.

 We've also tried to inject as much related information as possible for the various topics covered within, ranging from gotchas to other resources where one could explore subtopics in greater depth.

One aside: if you encounter a section explaining information you're already well-versed in, please bear with us as other readers may benefit from the discussion. We strive to keep the pace brisk, but we'd prefer not to leave any folks out.

How This Book Is Organized

Sinatra: Up and Running is organized as follows.

The Basics

Chapter 1, *Taking the Stage*, serves as a high-level introduction to some of the core concepts in Sinatra. It also discusses how to install the Sinatra gem, and walks through the creation of a simple application.

Chapter 2, *Fundamentals*, covers the different features of Sinatra, such as route definitions, creating views, managing sessions, and so on. It also serves as something of a reference chapter, with each topic discussed in granular fashion.

 If you've already built some Sinatra applications of your own and are fairly comfortable doing so, you can likely just skim through Chapters 1 and 2, although the newest release of Sinatra (version 1.3.1) contains a number of changes that are worth exploring (including support for the HTTP PATCH verb, streaming, etc.).

Digging Deeper

In Chapter 3, *A Peek Behind the Curtain*, we discuss the internals of Sinatra and its implementation; this includes coverage of Rack, building middleware, and other topics that clarify what really happens under the hood.

Chapter 4, *Modular Applications*, covers the various approaches available for subclassing Sinatra, allowing you to create significantly more flexible and robust architectures.

 If you've built some Sinatra applications but have never really explored the source code (or written Rack applications directly), this section will help to flesh out your knowledge. Understanding the modular application approach is critical to taking full advantage of what Sinatra offers.

Hands On

In Chapter 5, *Your Own Blog Engine*, we put the theory into application and create a Markdown-powered blog that takes advantage of the service hooks provided by the GitHub API.

Conventions Used in This Book

The following typographical conventions are used in this book:

Italic
> Indicates new terms, URLs, email addresses, filenames, and file extensions.

`Constant width`
> Used for program listings, as well as within paragraphs to refer to program elements such as variable or function names, databases, data types, environment variables, statements, and keywords.

`Constant width bold`
> Shows commands or other text that should be typed literally by the user.

Constant width italic

Shows text that should be replaced with user-supplied values or by values determined by context.

 This icon signifies a tip, suggestion, or general note.

 This icon indicates a warning or caution.

Using Code Examples

This book is here to help you get your job done. In general, you may use the code in this book in your programs and documentation. You do not need to contact us for permission unless you're reproducing a significant portion of the code. For example, writing a program that uses several chunks of code from this book does not require permission. Selling or distributing a CD-ROM of examples from O'Reilly books does require permission. Answering a question by citing this book and quoting example code does not require permission. Incorporating a significant amount of example code from this book into your product's documentation does require permission.

We appreciate, but do not require, attribution. An attribution usually includes the title, author, publisher, and ISBN. For example: "*Sinatra: Up and Running* by Alan Harris and Konstantin Haase (O'Reilly). Copyright 2012 O'Reilly Media, Inc., 978-1-449-30423-2."

If you feel your use of code examples falls outside fair use or the permission given above, feel free to contact us at *permissions@oreilly.com*.

Safari® Books Online

 Safari Books Online is an on-demand digital library that lets you easily search over 7,500 technology and creative reference books and videos to find the answers you need quickly.

With a subscription, you can read any page and watch any video from our library online. Read books on your cell phone and mobile devices. Access new titles before they are available for print, and get exclusive access to manuscripts in development and post feedback for the authors. Copy and paste code samples, organize your favorites, download chapters, bookmark key sections, create notes, print out pages, and benefit from tons of other time-saving features.

O'Reilly Media has uploaded this book to the Safari Books Online service. To have full digital access to this book and others on similar topics from O'Reilly and other publishers, sign up for free at *http://my.safaribooksonline.com*.

How to Contact Us

Please address comments and questions concerning this book to the publisher:

O'Reilly Media, Inc.
1005 Gravenstein Highway North
Sebastopol, CA 95472
800-998-9938 (in the United States or Canada)
707-829-0515 (international or local)
707-829-0104 (fax)

We have a web page for this book, where we list errata, examples, and any additional information. You can access this page at:

http://shop.oreilly.com/product/0636920019664.do

To comment or ask technical questions about this book, send email to:

bookquestions@oreilly.com

For more information about our books, courses, conferences, and news, see our website at *http://www.oreilly.com*.

Find us on Facebook: *http://facebook.com/oreilly*

Follow us on Twitter: *http://twitter.com/oreillymedia*

Watch us on YouTube: *http://www.youtube.com/oreillymedia*

## CHAPTER 1

Taking the Stage

To begin, let's take a moment to address a specific question: "what exactly is Sinatra?" We'll start with a somewhat broad, sweeping answer, and spend the remainder of our time together drilling down into the finer details.

Sinatra is a *domain-specific language* for building websites, web services, and web applications in Ruby. It emphasizes a minimalistic approach to development, offering only what is essential to handle HTTP requests and deliver responses to clients.

> At a high-level, a domain-specific language is one that is dedicated to solving a particular type of problem. For example, SQL (structured query language) is designed to facilitate interaction with relational database systems. By contrast, a general-purpose language such as Ruby can be used to write code in many different domains.
>
> This is a somewhat simplified view of things; if you're interested in delving deeper into the landscape of DSLs consider Martin Fowler's excellent "Domain-Specific Languages" (Addison-Wesley).

Written in less than 2,000 lines of Ruby, Sinatra's syntax (while expressive) is simple and straightforward. If you're looking to rapidly assemble an API, build a site with minimal fuss and setup, or create a Ruby-based web service, then Sinatra has quite a bit to offer. As we'll see later, Sinatra applications can also be embedded into other Ruby web applications, packaged as a gem for wider distribution, and so on.

In this chapter, our goal is to get off the ground as quickly as possible. We'll install Sinatra and a supporting web server to host our application, then create a simple app that responds to an HTTP request.

A quick disclaimer: at the outset, the code we present will not have much in the way of robust error handling. Instead we will focus purely on the syntax required to express core concepts without distraction. In discussing the fundamentals (particularly in Chapter 2), we will establish the built-in mechanisms that Sinatra provides for handling faults of varying nature.

Of course, normal Ruby best practices hold true; Avdi Grimm offers excellent coverage on the nuances of handling Ruby error conditions at *http://exceptionalruby.com/*.

Characteristics of Sinatra

We'll get into Sinatra's features and syntax in a moment; at the outset, it would be useful to define some parameters around what makes Sinatra distinctive and unique in the Ruby web ecosystem.

Is It a Framework?

Sinatra is not a framework; you'll find no built-in ORM (object-relational mapper) tools, no pre-fab configuration files...you won't even get a project folder unless you create one yourself.

While it may not seem like it now, this can be quite liberating. Sinatra applications are very flexible by nature, typically no larger than they need to be and can easily be distributed as gems.

A notable example along these lines is Resque, a very handy job processor created by the folks at GitHub. If you happen to install it, you'll find it comes with a Sinatra application that can be used to monitor the status of the jobs you create.

Does It Implement MVC?

Sinatra does not force you to adhere to the model-view-controller pattern, or any other pattern for that matter. It is a lightweight wrapper around Rack middleware and encourages a close relationship between service endpoints and the HTTP verbs, making it particularly ideal for web services and APIs (application programming interfaces).

Model-view-controller (specifically the Model2 variant common to the web) is a way of architecting applications that many web frameworks have adopted. Although these frameworks may have routing rules that are similar in some ways to Sinatra's routes, they typically also enforce them strictly with requirements on folder names and project hierarchies.

The Padrino Framework, available from *http://www.padrinorb.com/*, brings the Sinatra core into the MVC world. If you're a Rails developer and find you're missing some of the features it provides, you might want to give Padrino a try.

Who's Using It?

GitHub, Heroku, BBC, thoughtbot, Songbird, Engine Yard, and many others are active users of Sinatra in production environments. You can rest assured that by learning and implementing Sinatra you are working with a tested and proven solution that supports a scalable, responsive web experience.

Initially developed by Blake Mizerany, the continued development and support of Sinatra is provided by the team at Heroku.

What Does a Production Project Look Like?

Believe it or not, it's not uncommon to find entire Sinatra applications encapsulated in a single physical file. You can certainly build larger applications, and we'll cover some helpful ways to lay out applications throughout the course of the book.

There are two primary approaches to building Sinatra applications: *classic* and *modular*. They're similar, but with a few caveats: you cannot have multiple classic applications running in one Ruby process, and classic mode will add some methods to Object (which could be a problem if you want to ship your application as a gem). You can also create Sinatra apps on the fly, entirely in code, from within another application.

What's the difference between the two? Well, the quick answer is that in modular mode, you explicitly subclass Sinatra and build your application within that scope; in classic mode, you just require Sinatra and start defining endpoints. Both have their pros and cons, depending on your needs.

We're going to explore the classic style of Sinatra application first in this book, then dive a little deeper into Rack, modular applications, and so on. You'll have a good sense of both methods shortly.

What's the Catch?

All these benefits sound great, but it doesn't indicate that Sinatra is the correct choice for every web-facing application under the sun. If you're looking to build the next gigantic social network, you certainly *could* do it in Sinatra, but it would require considerably more wiring on your part compared to the conveniences provided by a framework (such as Rails or Padrino). The choice of tools becomes one of balance, and you'll need to make judgment calls based on the needs of the project.

Later in the book we will demonstrate ways to better organize projects as they grow in scope. Any application can get away from you if you let it, and Sinatra applications are no exception.

Are These Skills Transferrable?

Beyond the close relationship it has with the underlying web protocols, Sinatra has also inspired a number of tools in languages such as Microsoft .NET (Nancy), Perl (Dancer), Lua (Mercury), and quite a few more.

Investing time in learning Sinatra is not only beneficial by way of becoming better acclimated with the tools and protocols that power the web, but can also serve as a convenient springboard to grokking other languages.

Installation

Installing Sinatra is straightforward; from the command line, simply type **gem install sinatra**. At the time of this writing, the current version of Sinatra is 1.3.1.

 Earlier versions of Sinatra had some issues with the Ruby 1.9.*x* family. Since 1.2, Sinatra plays nicely with Ruby 1.9.2, but you should be aware of the potential for issues with older combinations.

Thin

The installation is brief and fairly unceremonious. When it's finished, we recommend you also install the Thin web server by typing **gem install thin**. Sinatra will automatically use Thin to handle communication with clients, if it is available.

Why Thin as opposed to other server options? Most Ruby web developers are familiar with WEBrick, a web server written entirely in Ruby. Zed Shaw later introduced Mongrel, which gained popularity as a faster and more stable platform for Ruby web applications. Thin continues this evolution by using code from Mongrel to parse HTTP requests but improves network I/O performance via EventMachine, which manages evented network communication. If Thin is not installed, Sinatra will first try to run with Mongrel, choosing WEBrick if Mongrel isn't available either.

Sinatra 1.3.1 adds a number of new features, notably support for streaming. At the moment, there is a known issue with WEBrick and streaming: the response from the server arrives at the client all at once. This is currently being addressed.

For Windows users: depending on the specifics of your environment, you may need to build Thin from source. To do so, you'll need to install a C compiler or opt for one of the Ruby development kit versions. You can certainly run Sinatra without Thin, but be aware that Thin is known to perform better under high load than both Mongrel and WEBrick.

Up and Running

It's painless to get a Sinatra application off the ground. Open the text editor of your choice and enter the code in Example 1-1. The syntax is readable, but we'll discuss the finer details in a moment.

Example 1-1. A simple Sinatra application

```
require 'sinatra'

get '/' do
  "Hello, world!"
end
```

Save this file as *server.rb*. Once you've done so, type **ruby server.rb** at the command prompt. You should be notified that Sinatra has taken the stage, as shown in Figure 1-1.

If you happen to still use Ruby 1.8 and you run into "no such file to load" exceptions, try **ruby -rubygems server.rb** instead. To avoid those extra characters, you can simply set the environment variable **RUBYOPT** to **-rubygems**. On Linux or Mac OS X, this can easily be done by adding **RUBYOPT=-rubygems** to your *.bashrc* in your home directory.

By default, the application will listen on port 4567. You can select any available port by typing **ruby server.rb -p *port_num***.

Open a web browser and navigate to *http://localhost:4567/*. Your Sinatra application should respond with the cheerful greeting displayed in Figure 1-2.

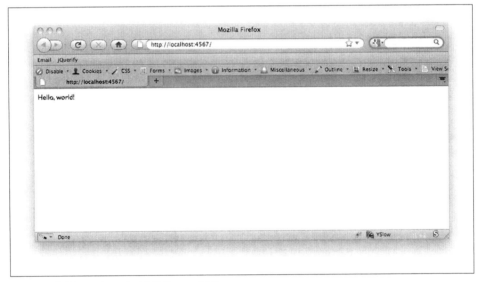

Figure 1-1. *Sinatra has taken the stage*

Figure 1-2. *The archetypical "Hello, world!"*

Breaking Down the Syntax

We've installed Sinatra and Thin, created a simple application, and verified that it responds properly to an HTTP GET request. So what's happening under the hood?

Sinatra is essentially a lightweight layer separating you as a developer from a piece of Ruby middleware called Rack. Rack wraps HTTP requests to help standardize communication between Ruby web applications and web servers. Sinatra abstracts Rack, allowing you to focus solely on responding to HTTP requests without worrying about the underlying plumbing.

The only aspect that should look foreign to the average Ruby developer is line 3:

```
get '/' do
```

Here we get our taste of the Sinatra DSL syntax, which is typically expressed in the form *verb 'route' do*. In our code, we are instructing the application to respond to HTTP GET requests to the path '/'; our response is composed by the block we provided for behavior. This composite endpoint is referred to as a *route*. Sinatra applications respond to one or more routes to provide their functionality.

This is part of the Sinatra magic; this code doesn't look like a typical method definition because in actuality, it's not. It's actually a method *call*.

Sinatra's base class defines a handful of public methods matching the HTTP verbs (which we'll discuss in depth in Chapter 2). The methods accept paths, options, and blocks. The block in Example 1-1 is the implicit return of "Hello, world!" and this is what gets evaluated deeper in the library. By making use of Ruby's flexible nature with regard to brackets and parentheses, Sinatra is able to provide a syntax that reads quite naturally.

It's definitely worth taking a tour of the Sinatra source code at *https:// github.com/sinatra/sinatra* when time permits.

Routes in your application are matched in top-down order; the first route that matches the incoming request is the one that gets used. This becomes an important point when we begin creating routes that include wildcards or other optional parameters where very different actions can occur depending on the values provided in the request. We'll revisit this point with concrete examples in Chapter 2.

This route is certainly on the simpler side of things; indeed the point is to demonstrate how little code it takes to create a "complete" application. More complex routes can respond to various HTTP verbs, contain wildcards, different types of pattern matches, and multiple routes can respond with the same action. We'll greatly expand on routes in Chapter 2.

Testing with Telnet

One critical key point when developing with Sinatra is that the program doesn't respond to *anything* you don't tell it to. We can see this quite clearly with a quick Telnet session, demonstrated in Example 1-2.

From the command line, type **telnet 0.0.0.0 4567** to establish a session with your application. Type the lines that are not italicized in the example below exactly as they appear. After the Host: 0.0.0.0 line, press return a second time. This ends the "headers" section, which we'll talk more about in the next chapter. For now it's sufficient to say that this tells the server you don't have anything further to say and it should start processing.

The lines that are italicized and indented are the responses from the web server. If you encounter any errors (such as the connection being closed) start Telnet again and ensure that each line is typed accurately.

Example 1-2. Sending HTTP messages to a Sinatra application using Telnet

```
[~]$ telnet 0.0.0.0 4567
GET / HTTP/1.1
Host: 0.0.0.0

    HTTP/1.1 200 OK
    Content-Type: text/html;charset=utf-8
    Content-Length: 13
    Connection: keep-alive
    Server: thin 1.2.10 codename I'm dumb

    Hello, world!
```

After connecting to the Sinatra application, we issued a GET request to the "/" route. The application promptly responded with our chipper greeting (and a tongue-in-cheek header identifying the codename for the latest version of Thin).

Thin releases typically have codenames like in the example above. For example, version 1.2.2 is named "I Find Your Lack of Sauce Disturbing."

What would happen if we were to issue a POST to the application? Let's give it a try; we'll POST the payload "foo=bar" to the "/" route.

The same rules apply; the non-italicized lines should be typed exactly as shown, there should be a blank line between Content-Length: 7 and foo=bar, and there should be a blank line after foo=bar.

```
POST / HTTP/1.1
Host: 0.0.0.0
Content-Length: 7

foo=bar
```

```
HTTP/1.1 404 Not Found
X-Cascade: pass
Content-Type: text/html;charset=utf-8
Content-Length: 410
Connection: keep-alive
Server: thin 1.2.10 codename I'm dumb

<!DOCTYPE html>
<html>
<head>
  <style type="text/css">
    body { text-align:center;font-family:helvetica,arial;font-size:22px;
       color:#888;margin:20px}
    #c {margin:0 auto;width:500px;text-align:left}
  </style>
</head>
<body>
  <h2>Sinatra doesn't know this ditty.</h2>
  <img src='/__sinatra__/404.png'>
  <div id="c">
    Try this:
    <pre>post '/' do
      "Hello World"
    end</pre>
  </div>
</body>
</html>
```

Yikes. This, however, is to be expected. Sinatra's "stay out of the way" approach carries with it the understanding that by staying out of the way, you are expected to pick up the slack. We'll learn how to do so in Chapter 2.

If you examine the response from the server, you'll notice it's an HTML page. Sinatra is pretty helpful; it noticed you were trying to issue a request with a verb it didn't recognize, so it's giving you a hint. More than a hint, really...it's flat-out telling you how you can make the error disappear. The visual form of this message is shown in Figure 1-3.

You don't have to address this now; it's just helpful to know that Sinatra typically chimes in with particularly useful information when routing is askew.

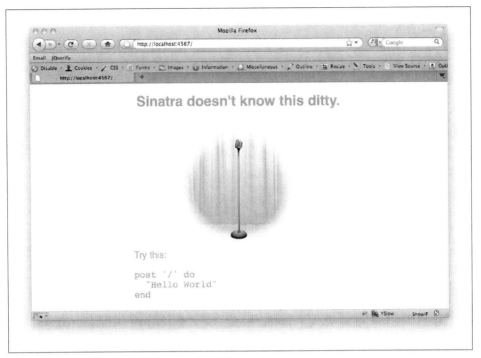

Figure 1-3. More than a stack trace, it's free software development

Rock, Paper, Scissors or "The Shape of Things to Come"

Web development can be so serious; let's take a moment to have a little fun and make a Sinatra application that will play rock, paper, scissors with us.

 We'll touch briefly on what's happening at each stage of the process, but don't worry too much about the particulars right now; the goal is just to whip up a quick little app. We'll cover all the concepts used shortly.

To begin, create a new file called game.rb in a folder of your choosing. We'll get the application rolling by defining a route; players will make requests to this route and provide the throw they'd like to make. Example 1-3 shows the starting point of our game.

Example 1-3. Starting the rock, paper, scissors application

```
require 'sinatra'

get '/throw/:type' do
```

```
  # play here
end
```

Now we should define the moves that are valid. We'll also specify that we're only returning plain old text (as opposed to HTML) when the player makes a move. The code to handle this is shown in Example 1-4.

Example 1-4. Specifying things that should happen prior to handling the request

```
require 'sinatra'

# before we process a route, we'll set the response as
# plain text and set up an array of viable moves that
# a player (and the computer) can perform
before do
  content_type :txt
  @defeat = {rock: :scissors, paper: :rock, scissors: :paper}
  @throws = @defeat.keys
end

get '/throw/:type' do
  # play here
end
```

Great, now we have a set of valid moves defined and our route will return plain text. Next, we should handle the input from the user and make sure it's valid by checking against @throws (see Example 1-5).

Example 1-5. Validating the user input

```
require 'sinatra'

# before we process a route, we'll set the response as
# plain text and set up an array of viable moves that
# a player (and the computer) can perform
before do
  content_type :txt
  @defeat = {rock: :scissors, paper: :rock, scissors: :paper}
  @throws = @defeat.keys
end

get '/throw/:type' do
  # the params[] hash stores querystring and form data.
  player_throw = params[:type].to_sym

  # in the case of a player providing a throw that is not valid,
  # we halt with a status code of 403 (Forbidden) and let them
  # know they need to make a valid throw to play.
  if !@throws.include?(player_throw)
    halt 403, "You must throw one of the following: #{@throws}"
  end
end
```

Now if a user tries to throw foobar, the application will inform her it's an invalid move and provide suitable options in return; processing will stop immediately when halt is called.

Next, let's get the computer to pick a random move and compare it to the user move. We'll provide some appropriate messages for each case (win, lose, and tie), as shown in Example 1-6.

Example 1-6. The final rock, paper, scissors application

```ruby
require 'sinatra'

# before we process a route, we'll set the response as
# plain text and set up an array of viable moves that
# a player (and the computer) can perform
before do
  content_type :txt
  @defeat = {rock: :scissors, paper: :rock, scissors: :paper}
  @throws = @defeat.keys
end

get '/throw/:type' do
  # the params[] hash stores querystring and form data.
  player_throw = params[:type].to_sym

  # in the case of a player providing a throw that is not valid,
  # we halt with a status code of 403 (Forbidden) and let them
  # know they need to make a valid throw to play.
  if !@throws.include?(player_throw)
    halt 403, "You must throw one of the following: #{@throws}"
  end

  # now we can select a random throw for the computer
  computer_throw = @throws.sample

  # compare the player and computer throws to determine a winner
  if player_throw == computer_throw
    "You tied with the computer. Try again!"
  elsif computer_throw == @defeat[player_throw]
    "Nicely done; #{player_throw} beats #{computer_throw}!"
  else
    "Ouch; #{computer_throw} beats #{player_throw}. Better luck next time!"
  end
end
```

And that's it! The game will let the player know if there's a tie, and if not it will compare the player and computer throws to determine whether the player won or lost.

Type **ruby game.rb** to start the game, then browse to *http://localhost:4567/throw/scissors* to try your luck against the machine. Figure 1-4 shows how well we fared.

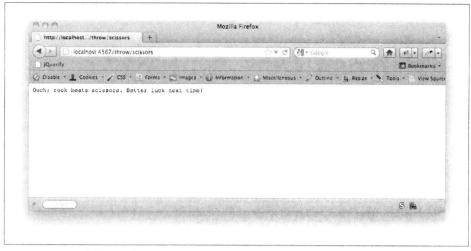

Figure 1-4. Hopefully your luck is a little better than ours

Summary

It should be obvious at this point that Sinatra has been designed with rapid development in mind. That said, there's a lot more to explore. So far, we've discussed what Sinatra is and what makes it distinctive from other Ruby web development tools. Next, we installed Sinatra as well as Thin, a web server to host our code locally. We also created a simple application that responds to a single route and saw how Sinatra handles missing routes. Finally, we created a game of rock, paper, scissors that pits human versus machine in a battle to the death.

Moving ahead, we'll take an in-depth look at Sinatra routing, how it maps to the HTTP specification, and discuss how to create more comprehensive applications.

## CHAPTER 2

Fundamentals

In Chapter 1, we created Sinatra applications that had a single *HTTP endpoint* exposed as a route. In this chapter, we'll explore the common HTTP verbs and their usage, how to construct more complex routes around those verbs, how to include static resources (such as raw HTML pages, stylesheets, images, and JavaScripts), and how to create dynamic HTML views. We'll also cover working with HTTP headers, configuration blocks, and filters.

This chapter will be the most "reference-y" of the book, with each topic covered using the briefest examples possible to avoid cluttering the discussion with unrelated facets. The next few chapters will delve into the more theoretical and architectural aspects of Sinatra, then we'll turn our attention to practical application and create several projects that are more involved and cover a wider breadth of knowledge.

Routing

The core of any Sinatra application is the ability to respond to one or more routes. Routes are the primary way that users interact with your application. To understand how Sinatra handles routing, we must first examine HTTP, the Hypertext Transfer Protocol.

The discussion takes place from the perspective of the server; a *request* is created by a client (which may be a browser, another web application, etc.), and a *response* is created by the server and sent back.

This is also true with regard to operating on request and response objects in Sinatra, which we will discuss throughout this chapter; the former will contain properties related to the client speaking to the server (such as location headers, cookie data, etc.), and the latter will contain information for the client to parse (such as content length, how long to cache something, and so on).

Hypertext Transfer Protocol

The HTTP specification is a network protocol that makes up the backbone of communication on the Internet between clients and servers.

When a client (which might be a web browser, a web application, a service, etc.) wants to interact with a web server over HTTP, it composes a *message*. An HTTP message is plain-text and line-oriented, making it very straightforward to construct and inspect. We saw this briefly in Chapter 1 when we composed requests to our application using Telnet.

Likewise, when a server is done processing a request, it can communicate information back to the client by creating its own HTTP message. The message usually contains information such as the status (did the client request succeed, was there an error in processing the request, etc.), what type of content is being sent back (plain text, an image, HTML, etc.) and other data which we'll discuss throughout this chapter.

A message has the following characteristics, in order:

Start line
> The start line is the first line in the request. It defines the *HTTP verb* to use, what resource to access, and denotes what version of HTTP is being used so that the server knows how to parse the request properly.

Headers
> Headers provide additional information about the request. There are a number of standard headers that cover needs such as describing the length of the message, including the values of any cookies for that domain, and so on. It's also possible to define custom headers that aren't included in the HTTP specification.

> It's not required to have headers in an HTTP message. Any included headers have a name and a value, separated by a single colon. Each header is on its own line, and the headers section ends with a blank line.

Message body
> The message body is the last item in the HTTP message, and it can contain any binary or text data. For example, when you upload an image to your favorite social network, the binary data for that image is stored in the message body and read by the server.

> A message body is not required in an HTTP message.

Verbs

As mentioned, the start line of an HTTP message includes a verb. This defines the type of request being made and therefore how the server will interpret it; for instance, a GET will be treated very differently than a PUT (or at least it *should* be!).

For most development purposes, we can focus on five commonly-used verbs.

GET

A GET request is used to ask a server to return a representation of a resource. For example, when you browse to *http://www.google.com/* the browser will issue a GET request; the server will (hopefully!) respond with the markup necessary for your browser to render the page markup. Additional resources (images, stylesheets, scripts, etc.) are requested by the browser as further GETs.

POST

A POST is used to submit data to a web server. Arguably the most ubiquitous example of a POST is the humble login form. A user fills in his credentials, clicks a button, and the browser submits the data via a POST to the server. The server can then respond accordingly based on the payload.

PUT

PUT is used to create or update a representation of a resource on a server. If you were in the process of adding photos to an online album, you could create PUT requests that contain the complete contents of the resource, which would then be available at a unique URL on the server.

The line between POST and PUT blurs slightly in practice; the real difference between the two verbs lies in how the server should handle the payload. If the request is a POST, the current URL *may* handle payload application, but if the request is a PUT the supplied location *must* be what handles it.

In simpler terms, you might POST some data to a form that is designed to accept a variety of input and apply it to one or more resources in your application. Your POST indicates what location on the server will handle the process, but doesn't necessarily map to any one particular resource. A PUT request, by contrast, should refer to one (and only one) resource in particular.

If it's still unclear, you can find a more in-depth discussion at *http://www.w3.org/Protocols/rfc2616/rfc2616-sec9.html*.

DELETE

DELETE is used to destroy a resource on a server.

In practice, although PUT and DELETE have unique identities, their functionality is often expressed via POSTs in web applications. The reason is fairly mundane: the HTML `<form>` element supports only GET and POST as available actions.

Some frameworks circumvent this by providing a hidden `<input>` field whose value represents the verb to use, and you can certainly use the other verbs via JavaScript and client libraries.

GET, PUT, and DELETE are expected to exhibit what is termed *idempotence*: an action that is idempotent should deliver identical results if the action is repeated. POST is not considered idempotent as repeated POST requests may continually update the server and return different results.

PATCH

PATCH is used to update a portion of a resource; this is in contrast to PUT, which replaces it wholesale.

PATCH is *not* required to be idempotent, as it is conceivable that partial resource updates may require a known starting point or risk corruption.

RFC 5789 contains additional helpful information on the semantics of the PATCH verb; you can investigate further at *http://tools .ietf.org/html/rfc5789*.

PATCH is new to Sinatra as of version 1.3.0; if you try to create a route that responds to it in earlier versions, you will be rewarded with an `undefined method` exception.

The HTTP specification defines several verbs we won't be specifically discussing here: OPTIONS, HEAD, TRACE, and CONNECT (of which the last two are not natively supported by Sinatra). These fulfill various functions, such as returning headers, enumerating options on the server, and so on.

Collectively, these verbs make up the vocabulary that Sinatra uses to express the definition of a route. There are a variety of ways to configure routes in Sinatra; we'll examine both the common and the more esoteric. Regardless of their individual semantics, all route forms revolve around the HTTP verbs and follow a general pattern.

Common Route Definition

We saw the basic type of route definition in the sample application in Chapter 1. To declare a route in Sinatra, you must supply the HTTP verb to respond to, the specific URL, and then optionally define the behavior desired for the route. See Example 2-1 for the common form of route definition.

Example 2-1. The common form of route definition

```
require 'sinatra'

get '/' do
  "Triggered via GET"
```

```
end

post '/' do
  "Triggered via POST"
end

put '/' do
  "Triggered via PUT"
end

delete '/' do
  "Triggered via DELETE"
end

patch '/' do
  "Triggered via PATCH"
end

options '/' do
  "Triggered via OPTIONS"
end
```

There are a number of extensions to Sinatra available in the `sinatra-contrib` project on GitHub. One of them, `Sinatra::MultiRoute`, allows for the creation of routes with verbs not normally supported by Sinatra (among other things).

The project can be found at *https://github.com/sinatra/sinatra-contrib*.

Many URLs, Similar Behaviors

Sometimes you may encounter situations where multiple routes should respond the same way. We're always trying to keep our code *DRY*, and luckily there is an approach that comes in handy without being unwieldy; Example 2-2 demonstrates how to respond to an array of routes by verb.

DRY stands for "Don't Repeat Yourself"; it's also occasionally expressed as DIE, or "Duplication is Evil."

Example 2-2. Many URLs sharing a handler

```
require 'sinatra'

['/one', '/two', '/three'].each do |route|
  get route do
      "Triggered #{route} via GET"
  end

  post route do
```

```
      "Triggered #{route} via POST"
  end

  put route do
      "Triggered #{route} via PUT"
  end

  delete route do
      "Triggered #{route} via DELETE"
  end

  patch route do
      "Triggered #{route} via PATCH"
  end
end
```

 Notice that the URLs in Example 2-2 do not have trailing slashes. In fact, if you try to browse to *http://localhost:4567/one/*, it won't work.

If you'd like to make the trailing slash optional, simply add a slash and a question mark to the end of the URL.

```
      get('/one/?') { ... }
```

Routes with Parameters

Routes in Sinatra can also accept parameters that are exposed in code via the `params` array, as shown in Example 2-3.

Example 2-3. Accessing parameters in the request

```
require 'sinatra'

get '/:name' do
  "Hello, #{params[:name]}!"
end
```

In the case of data submission requests, the data in the payload is available in the `params` array. Unlike GET and DELETE requests, you don't need to specify the payload parameters in the URL. Example 2-4 shows this in practice.

Example 2-4. Data payloads are stored in the usual array.

```
require 'sinatra'

post '/login' do
  username = params[:username]
  password = params[:password]
end

put '/users/:id' do
  # let's assume we could retrieve a User
  u = User.find(params[:id])
```

```
    u.first_name = params[:first_name]
    u.last_name = params[:last_name]
    u.save
end
```

Routes with Query String Parameters

In addition to parameters that are used to compose the URL itself, Sinatra also stores query string parameters by name in the `params` array. See Example 2-5.

Example 2-5. Retrieving query string parameters

```
require 'sinatra'

get '/:name' do
  # assumes a URL in the form /some_name?foo=XYZ
  "You asked for #{params[:name]} as well as #{params[:foo]}"
end
```

Routes with Wildcards

Routes in Sinatra can also accept wildcards in the form of the "splat" (*) character, as demonstrated in Example 2-6. Anything passed in the wildcard position is stored in `params[:splat]`, which itself contains an array.

Example 2-6. Using wildcards in a route

```
require 'sinatra'

get '/*' do
  "You passed in #{params[:splat]}"
end
```

The route described in Example 2-6 is a greedy match; for example, if you run the code and browse to *http://localhost:4567/foo/bar*, the output on the screen will be `You passed in ["foo/bar"]`. If you browse to *http://localhost:4567/foo/bar/baz/bop*, the output will be `You passed in ["foo/bar/baz/bop"]`.

This brings us to a very important Sinatra routing tenet. It's a simple rule, but critical to emphasize, especially as we move into static files and views.

The First Sufficient Match Wins

When Sinatra parses routes, the first sufficient match is the one that will be executed. This is true even when there is a better or more specific route definition later in the file. Let's take a look at a route configuration in Example 2-7, where a greedy match eats up a more specific one.

Example 2-7. Demonstrating Sinatra's "first sufficient match" approach

```
require 'sinatra'

get '/*' do
  "NOM NOM NOM"
end

get '/specific' do
  "You'll never, ever see me."
end
```

Browsing to *http://localhost:4567/specific* should return NOM NOM NOM even though there is a better match later in the file. It is an easily avoidable problem, but very important to bear in mind when working with a complex set of route definitions.

Sinatra also allows us to include static resources in our applications, such as CSS files, JavaScripts, images, and HTML files.

Pop quiz time! Let's say we have a static file called *public.html* that contains the text "This is a static file", and we *also* define a route in the form get('/public.html') { "This is delivered via the route." }.

Given that we have two definitions for the same resource, what will be displayed when browsing to *http://localhost:4567/public.html*? We'll discuss the answer in just a moment.

Routes with Regular Expressions

Sinatra also accepts regular expressions as a way to match incoming requests to particular handlers. Because of their flexible nature, we'll also use Example 2-8 to reinforce the dangers of greedy matches.

Example 2-8. Careless regular expressions can lead to greedy bugs

```
require 'sinatra'

get %r{/(sp|gr)eedy} do
  "You got caught in the greedy route!"
end

get '/speedy' do
  "No one calls me :("
end

get '/greedy' do
  "No one calls me either!"
end
```

As we're sure you can guess, the regular expression match is the first sufficient match in comparison to the routes defined later, and therefore the later routes will not be executed. This isn't to say that using regular expressions to match routes is a bad idea.

We just mean to convey that some caution should be exercised (as well as for wildcard matches).

Halting a Request

Sometimes we don't want an operation to continue; maybe a critical error has occurred, or perhaps a process is taking too long and we'd like to bail out. Sinatra provides a halt method for just this purpose as shown in Example 2-9.

Example 2-9. Using halt to stop a request

```
require 'sinatra'

get '/halt' do
  'You will not see this output.'
  halt 500
end
```

Now let's use cURL to see what happens when this route is executed:

```
$ curl -v http://localhost:4567/halt
* About to connect() to localhost port 4567 (#0)
*   Trying 127.0.0.1... connected
* Connected to localhost (127.0.0.1) port 4567 (#0)
> GET /halt HTTP/1.1
> User-Agent: curl/7.21.2 (x86_64-apple-darwin10.4.0)
> Host: localhost:4567
> Accept: */*
>
< HTTP/1.1 500 Internal Server Error
< Connection: close
< Date: Sat, 17 Sep 2011 21:09:42 GMT
< Content-Type: text/html;charset=utf-8
< Content-Length: 0
<
* Closing connection #0
```

A status code of "500 Internal Server Error" was returned, and the text we entered was not delivered to the client (further verified by a Content-Length header of value 0).

Passing a Request

Depending on the structure of your application, there may be instances where you'd like to pass processing on to the next best matching route (if available). To do so, simply define the criteria on which to match, and use the pass method to look for the next available match. See Example 2-10.

Example 2-10. Passing to another matching route

```
require 'sinatra'

before do
```

```
  content_type :txt
end

get %r{/(sp|gr)eedy} do
  pass if request.path =~ /\/speedy/
  "You got caught in the greedy route!"
end

get '/speedy' do
  "You must have passed to me!"
end
```

Now, if a user requests "/speedy", she will actually reach the regular expression-based route handler first, then be passed along to the latter handler:

```
$ curl http://localhost:4567/greedy
  You got caught in the greedy route!
```

```
$ curl http://localhost:4567/speedy
  You must have passed to me!
```

Redirecting a Request

You can redirect a request to a different location using the redirect method. Optionally, you can provide a status code as shown in Example 2-11(to differentiate between a temporary and permanent redirection, for example).

Example 2-11. Redirect a request with optional status codes

```
require 'sinatra'

get '/redirect' do
  redirect 'http://www.google.com'
end

get '/redirect2' do
  redirect 'http://www.google.com', 301
end
```

Let's examine these routes via cURL again to see the difference that the status codes make:

```
$ curl -v http://localhost:4567/redirect
* About to connect() to localhost port 4567 (#0)
*   Trying 127.0.0.1... connected
* Connected to localhost (127.0.0.1) port 4567 (#0)
> GET /redirect HTTP/1.1
> User-Agent: curl/7.21.2 (x86_64-apple-darwin10.4.0)
> Host: localhost:4567
> Accept: */*
>
< HTTP/1.1 302 Moved Temporarily
< Connection: close
< Date: Sat, 17 Sep 2011 21:27:45 GMT
```

```
< Content-Type: text/html;charset=utf-8
< Location: http://www.google.com
< Content-Length: 0
<
* Closing connection #0

$ curl -v http://localhost:4567/redirect2
* About to connect() to localhost port 4567 (#0)
*   Trying 127.0.0.1... connected
* Connected to localhost (127.0.0.1) port 4567 (#0)
> GET /redirect2 HTTP/1.1
> User-Agent: curl/7.21.2 (x86_64-apple-darwin10.4.0)
> Host: localhost:4567
> Accept: */*
>
< HTTP/1.1 301 Moved Permanently
< Connection: close
< Date: Sat, 17 Sep 2011 21:27:47 GMT
< Content-Type: text/html;charset=utf-8
< Location: http://www.google.com
< Content-Length: 0
<
* Closing connection #0
```

By default, if you do not provide a status code to the `redirect` method, it will assume
you want a temporary redirection (code 302). This indicates to clients that they would
normally find the resource they were looking for at the requested URL, but for the
moment it is available elsewhere. A 301 redirection tells the client that the URL they
requested may have been correct in the past, but the current location is elsewhere (and
in the future, the client should only request that new location).

Static Files

As Sinatra developers, we're not bound to route creation as a way to deliver static
content. In Examples 2-12 and 2-13, assume that we have a subfolder named "public"
that contains a single file, *public.html*.

Example 2-12. A simple HTML file

```
<!DOCTYPE html>
<html>
  <head>
    <meta charset="UTF-8">
    <title>Static file</title>
  </head>
  <body>
    <h1>This is a static file.</h1>
  </body>
</html>
```

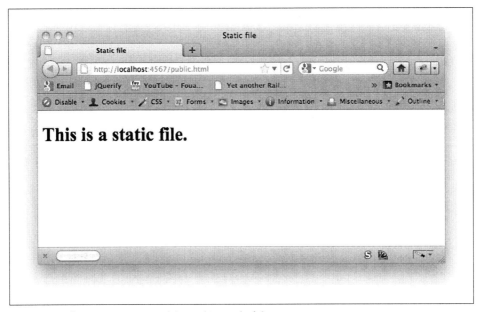

Figure 2-1. The static resource is delivered instead of the route content

Example 2-13. A Sinatra application with a route conflict

```
require 'sinatra'

get '/public.html' do
  'This is delivered via the route.'
end
```

Earlier we posed the question of what would be delivered to the client in the event that a defined route conflicted with the name of a static resource. The answer to that question is shown in Figure 2-1.

You'll notice that the "public" folder is omitted from the URL. In the case of static files, views, and so on, the folder is assumed and not included in any public-facing component. For example, a folder called "javascripts" inside the "public" folder would be accessible through *http://localhost:4567/javascripts*.

> If you'd like to use a different location than "public" for your static resources, you're free to do so (although most applications simply use the default convention). You can swap the location with `set :pub lic_folder, File.dirname(__FILE__) + '/your_custom_location'`.
>
> This and several other configuration settings that we will call out in this chapter should be placed in a special block known as the `configure` block. We'll discuss how to use it shortly.

In older versions of Sinatra, the symbol was `:public` rather than `:pub lic_folder`; this has changed in 1.3.0 to help avoid collisions with Ruby's built-in `public` keyword. The `:public` symbol will still work, but it will offer up a warning: `:public is no longer used to avoid over loading Module#public`.

Views

Views in Sinatra are HTML templates that can optionally contain data passed from the application. There are numerous template engines available; Erb, Haml, and Erubis are just a few. We'll use Erb for our templates as it's fairly ubiquitous in the Ruby community these days, although any mature engine will do just fine as the usage is essentially the same in all cases.

Erb is also the template engine of choice for Rails, and David Heinemeier Hansson (author of the Rails framework) has indicated that this is unlikely to change any time soon.

There are two ways to interact with views in Sinatra: inline templates and external templates.

Inline Templates

Inline templates, unsurprisingly, are defined in the application code file itself. They are located at the bottom of the file; Example 2-14 shows how to include templates directly in your application files.

You can also have inline templates defined in other files, although by default only the ones in the application file get automatically loaded. You'll need to call `enable :inline_templates` in a `configure` block to bring in the others.

Example 2-14. Defining an Erb template using the inline approach

```
require 'sinatra'

get '/index' do
  erb :index
end

__END__

@@index

<!DOCTYPE html>
```

```
<html>
  <head>
    <meta charset="UTF-8">
    <title>Inline template</title>
  </head>
  <body>
    <h1>Worked!</h1>
  </body>
</html>
```

It's important to note that the name of the view *must* be a symbol. Inline templates require that you create a class variable of the same name so that Sinatra knows which template to render.

External View Files

Things can get pretty cluttered if you're relying solely on inline templates for your view needs. If you'd prefer to store your views externally, Sinatra will look for them by default in the "views" subfolder. In Example 2-15, a symbol containing the filename (up to the extension) is passed as the parameter for rendering. Example 2-16 shows a simple Erb file that will be rendered by the route.

 As with static resources, you can change the location of your views: `set :views, File.dirname(__FILE__) + '/your_custom_location'`. This is defined in the `configure` block.

Example 2-15. The Erb template has been extracted

```
require 'sinatra'

get '/index' do
  erb :index
end
```

Example 2-16. The contents of index.erb

```
<!DOCTYPE html>
<html>
  <head>
    <meta charset="UTF-8">
    <title>External template</title>
  </head>
  <body>
    <h1>Worked!</h1>
  </body>
</html>
```

External Views in Subfolders

In the spirit of reducing clutter, we may not always want all our external templates plopped into one folder. To reference views in subfolders, we need to convert a string representation of the path to a symbol. There are two ways to do this, both of which are demonstrated in Example 2-17.

Example 2-17. Referencing a view in a subfolder

```
require 'sinatra'

get '/:user/profile' do
  erb '/user/profile'.to_sym
end

get '/:user/help' do
  erb :'/user/help'
end
```

This code will look for files called *profile.erb* and *help.erb* in "/views/user". Either approach for creating the symbol is acceptable. Anecdotally, the use of #to_sym seems to be more common in practice.

 If you want to get technical, one could also use #intern as well.

Passing Data into Views

Information constructed in the back-end of the application can be shared to the front-end view through the use of instance variables, as shown in Examples 2-18 and 2-19.

Example 2-18. Creating instance variables for use in a view

```
require 'sinatra'

get '/home' do
  @name = 'Random User'
  erb :home
end
```

Example 2-19. Accessing instance variables in a view

```
<!DOCTYPE html>
<html>
<head>
  <meta charset="UTF-8">
  <title>Using instance variables</title>
</head>
<body>
  <h1>Hello, <%= @name %>!</h1>
```

```
</body>
</html>
```

Statements to be evaluated (displaying instance variables, performing transformation operations, etc.) are wrapped in <%= %> tags, while control statements (loops, etc.) are wrapped in <% %> tags. Example 2-20 shows how to create instance variables for use in a view, while Example 2-21 demonstrates the consumption of those variables (as well as the difference between evaluated and control statements in Erb).

Example 2-20. Iterating over a loop in a view

```
require 'sinatra'

get '/home' do
  @users = ['Sally', 'Jerry', 'Rocko']
  erb :home
end
```

Example 2-21. Accessing instance variables in a view using a loop

```
<!DOCTYPE html>
<html>
<head>
  <meta charset="UTF-8">
  <title>Using instance variables</title>
</head>
<body>
  <% @users.each do |user| %>
    <p><%= user %></p>
  <% end %>
</body>
</html>
```

Filters

Sinatra supports filters as a way to modify requests and responses, both before and after a route has been executed; Example 2-22 uses a before filter to set an instance variable prior to processing a route.

Example 2-22. Using before and after filters

```
require 'sinatra'

before do
  @before_value = 'foo'
end

get '/' do
  "before_value has been set to #{@before_value}"
end

after do
```

```
2. ~/work/oreilly/sinatra/new_code/ch_02 (ruby)
[ch_02]$ ruby app.rb
== Sinatra/1.2.6 has taken the stage on 4567 for development with backup from Thin
>> Thin web server (v1.2.11 codename Bat-Shit Crazy)
>> Maximum connections set to 1024
>> Listening on 0.0.0.0:4567, CTRL+C to stop
After filter called to perform some task.
127.0.0.1 - - [29/Aug/2011 11:37:49] "GET / HTTP/1.1" 200 32 0.0043
```

Figure 2-2. The static resource is delivered instead of the route content

```
  puts "After filter called to perform some task."
end
```

The after filter output is shown in Figure 2-2, where "After filter called to perform some task." has been displayed in the output stream.

> The before and after filters are identical in form to the route methods; specifically, you can provide a URL to a filter and Sinatra will match it.
>
> ```
> before('/index') { ... } # executed only before the '/index' route
> ```
>
> If you do not supply a URL (as shown in Example 2-22) the block will be executed before or after every request respectively.

Handling Errors

Anyone who has spent a significant amount of time writing code (especially for the web) can tell you that despite our best intentions, sometimes things go wrong. Two common problems in web applications are in the *400 and 500 error ranges*.

The HTTP specification defines a number of ranges that indicate the type of response that a server is sending to a client. For example, the 200–299 range is reserved for responses that indicate success in processing a request; this may involve creating a resource, returning markup, or similar tasks. By contrast, the 500–599 range is reserved for server errors, where processing was interrupted because of some unrecoverable condition on the application's side of the conversation (assuming that the client delivered a valid request).

Sinatra wraps up two common problems with helpers: *404 (Not Found)* and *500 (Internal Server Error)*.

These helpers are in the same context as normal routes and before filters, and can therefore enjoy the same conveniences; this includes rendering engine shortcuts (such as erb), the request and response objects, and so on.

404 Not Found

To easily handle the absence of a route or resource matching a particular request, you can render some form of output via the not_found block, as shown in Example 2-23.

Example 2-23. Gracefully handling 404 errors

```
require 'sinatra'

    before do
      content_type :txt
    end

    not_found do
      "Whoops! You requested a route that wasn't available."
    end
```

Now, since there are no conventional routes defined, any requests will be handled by the not_found call.

```
    $ curl -v http://localhost:4567/foo
    * About to connect() to localhost port 4567 (#0)
    *   Trying 127.0.0.1... connected
    * Connected to localhost (127.0.0.1) port 4567 (#0)
    > GET /foo HTTP/1.1
    > User-Agent: curl/7.19.7 (universal-apple-darwin10.0)
    > Host: localhost:4567
    > Accept: */*
    >
    < HTTP/1.1 404 Not Found
    < X-Frame-Options: sameorigin
    < X-XSS-Protection: 1; mode=block
    < Content-Type: text/html;charset=utf-8
    < X-Cascade: pass
    < Content-Length: 52
    < Connection: keep-alive
    < Server: thin 1.2.11 codename Bat-Shit Crazy
    <
    * Connection #0 to host localhost left intact
    * Closing connection #0
    Whoops! You requested a route that wasn't available.
```

500 Internal Server Error

In the event that an unhandled exception occurs while processing a request, you can handle it by defining an error block, as shown in Example 2-24.

Example 2-24. Gracefully handling 500 errors

```ruby
require 'sinatra'

  before do
    content_type :txt
  end

  configure do
    set :show_exceptions, false
  end

  get '/div_by_zero' do
    0 / 0
    "You won't see me."
  end

  error do
    "Y U NO WORK?"
  end
```

The "/div_by_zero" has an obvious unhandled exception in the division by zero operation. When encountered, this will result in the output of the **error** block being returned to the client.

 A logical question to ask is, "What happens if an unhandled exception occurs in the error-handling block?" The answer is that nothing will be returned to the client; the response will be totally empty (no headers, no body, etc.).

```
$ curl -v http://localhost:4567/div_by_zero
* About to connect() to localhost port 4567 (#0)
*   Trying 127.0.0.1... connected
* Connected to localhost (127.0.0.1) port 4567 (#0)
> GET /div_by_zero HTTP/1.1
> User-Agent: curl/7.19.7 (universal-apple-darwin10.0)
> Host: localhost:4567
> Accept: */*
>
< HTTP/1.1 500 Internal Server Error
< X-Frame-Options: sameorigin
< X-XSS-Protection: 1; mode=block
< Content-Type: text/plain;charset=utf-8
< Content-Length: 12
< Connection: keep-alive
< Server: thin 1.2.11 codename Bat-Shit Crazy
<
* Connection #0 to host localhost left intact
* Closing connection #0
Y U NO WORK?
```

Configuration

For your configuration needs, Sinatra makes available a method called `configure` that can be used globally or for specific routes or environments.

In the code shown in Example 2-25, the `configure` block is used to register a new *MIME type* in the form of a symbol, `:plain`. Next, a `before` block sets the content type that will be used to render a response for the route *http://localhost:4567/plain-text*. While the *http://localhost:4567/html* route will return HTML content, the *http://localhost: 4567/plain-text* route will return only text, which the browser will not render or style.

 MIME is short for Multipurpose Internet Mail Extensions. MIME types are standard ways of indicating to clients how to interpret or handle a particular piece of content. They were initially developed with regard to email clients, but have since expanded into other application types (such as web browsers).

Example 2-25. Using a configure block

```
require 'sinatra'

configure do
  mime_type :plain, 'text/plain'
end

before '/plain-text' do
  content_type :plain
end

get '/html' do
  '<h1>You should see HTML rendered.</h1>'
end

get '/plain-text' do
  '<h1>You should see plain text rendered.</h1>'
end
```

HTTP Headers

HTTP requests and responses are associated with a number of headers that provide additional information to clients and servers. For example, there are headers that are used to denote how long something should be cached, how long the content is, and so on. It's also possible to create custom headers of your own.

The headers Method

Sinatra provides a method called **headers** that can be used to set HTTP headers in your responses, which is demonstrated in Example 2-26. It accepts a hash where the key is the name of the header.

Example 2-26. Setting custom HTTP headers

```
require 'sinatra'

before do
  content_type :txt
end

get '/' do
  headers "X-Custom-Value" => "This is a custom HTTP header."
  'Custom header set'
end

get '/multiple' do
  headers "X-Custom-Value" => "foo", "X-Custom-Value-2" => "bar"
  'Multiple custom headers set'
end
```

You can check these headers with a quick run via cURL.

```
$ curl -v localhost:4567/
* About to connect() to localhost port 4567 (#0)
*   Trying 127.0.0.1... connected
* Connected to localhost (127.0.0.1) port 4567 (#0)
> GET / HTTP/1.1
> User-Agent: curl/7.19.7 (universal-apple-darwin10.0)
> Host: localhost:4567
> Accept: */*
>
< HTTP/1.1 200 OK
< Content-Type: text/plain;charset=utf-8
< X-Custom-Value: This is a custom HTTP header.
< Content-Length: 17
< Connection: keep-alive
< Server: thin 1.2.11 codename Bat-Shit Crazy
<
* Connection #0 to host localhost left intact
* Closing connection #0

$ curl -v localhost:4567/multiple
* About to connect() to localhost port 4567 (#0)
*   Trying 127.0.0.1... connected
* Connected to localhost (127.0.0.1) port 4567 (#0)
> GET /multiple HTTP/1.1
> User-Agent: curl/7.19.7 (universal-apple-darwin10.0)
> Host: localhost:4567
> Accept: */*
>
< HTTP/1.1 200 OK
```

```
< Content-Type: text/plain;charset=utf-8
< X-Custom-Value: foo
< X-Custom-Value-2: bar
< Content-Length: 27
< Connection: keep-alive
< Server: thin 1.2.11 codename Bat-Shit Crazy
<
* Connection #0 to host localhost left intact
* Closing connection #0
```

 The HTTP specification defines a number of standard headers; the generally-accepted convention is to prefix custom or user-defined headers with "X-", such as X-Custom-Value. There are several non-standard headers that are in common use: X-Forwarded-For, X-Requested-With, and X-Powered-By are just a few.

The standard HTTP headers can be found at *http://www.w3.org/Proto cols/rfc2616/rfc2616-sec14.html*.

Exploring the request Object

Sinatra exposes a variety of request information via the **request** object, as seen in Example 2-27. The **request** object holds a hash of request data such as who made the request, what version of the HTTP standard to use, and so on. We'll discuss the underlying mechanics of this object further when we delve into Rack in Chapter 3.

Example 2-27. Accessing request data

```
require 'sinatra'

before do
  content_type :txt
end

get '/' do
  request.env.map { |e| e.to_s + "\n" }
end
```

This application will iterate over all the values in the @env variable and display them as output.

```
$ curl http://localhost:9393/
["GATEWAY_INTERFACE", "CGI/1.1"]
["PATH_INFO", "/"]
["QUERY_STRING", ""]
["REMOTE_ADDR", "127.0.0.1"]
["REMOTE_HOST", "localhost"]
["REQUEST_METHOD", "GET"]
["REQUEST_URI", "http://localhost:9393/"]
["SCRIPT_NAME", ""]
["SERVER_NAME", "localhost"]
["SERVER_PORT", "9393"]
```

```
["SERVER_PROTOCOL", "HTTP/1.1"]
["SERVER_SOFTWARE", "WEBrick/1.3.1 (Ruby/1.9.2/2011-07-09)"]
["HTTP_USER_AGENT", "curl/7.19.7 (universal-apple-darwin10.0)"]
["HTTP_HOST", "localhost:9393"]
["HTTP_ACCEPT", "*/*"]
["rack.version", [1, 1]]
["rack.input", #<Rack::Lint::InputWrapper:0x0000010327f368 @input=#<StringIO:
0x000001009c8500>>]
["rack.errors", #<Rack::Lint::ErrorWrapper:0x0000010327f2f0 @error=#<IO:<STDERR>>>]
["rack.multithread", true]
["rack.multiprocess", false]
["rack.run_once", false]
["rack.url_scheme", "http"]
["HTTP_VERSION", "HTTP/1.1"]
["REQUEST_PATH", "/"]
["rack.request.query_string", ""]
["rack.request.query_hash", {}]
```

Similarly, we can iterate over the methods defined for the **request** object for comparison
purposes. See Example 2-28.

Example 2-28. Enumerating the methods on the request object

```ruby
require 'sinatra'

before do
  content_type :txt
end

get '/' do
  request.methods.map { |m| m.to_s + "\n" }
end
```

We've truncated the rendered output for brevity, but you'll see a number of the **@env**
fields represented.

```
$ curl localhost:4567/
accept
preferred_type
accept?
secure?
forwarded?
safe?
idempotent?
env
body
script_name
path_info
request_method
query_string
content_length
content_type
session
session_options
logger
```

```
media_type
media_type_params
content_charset
scheme
ssl?
referer
referrer
user_agent
cookies
xhr?
base_url
url
path
fullpath
accept_encoding
ip
parse_query
parse_multipart
```

Caching

Caching in web applications can be a complex topic, spanning a variety of tiers. Browsers, proxies, servers, and other devices can all cache content and resources independently. There are a number of HTTP headers that can be used to inform consumers of how to handle content; we'll examine a few here.

 For the purposes of this conversation, we can assume that "caching" refers to control provided by HTTP headers and is not inclusive of external services such as Memcached.

Setting Headers Manually

Using the headers helper we discussed earlier, you can set any desired headers to influence downstream caching. The code in Example 2-29 will inform consumers that the content should be cached for one hour.

Example 2-29. Setting cache headers manually

```
require 'sinatra'

before do
  content_type :txt
end

get '/' do
  headers "Cache-Control" => "public, must-revalidate, max-age=3600",
          "Expires" => Time.at(Time.now.to_i + (60 * 60)).to_s
  "This page rendered at #{Time.now}."
end
```

If you visit this page in a browser, refreshing will not update the time displayed on the page. The headers are shown in the cURL session below.

```
$ curl -v http://localhost:9393/
* About to connect() to localhost port 9393 (#0)
*   Trying 127.0.0.1... connected
* Connected to localhost (127.0.0.1) port 9393 (#0)
> GET / HTTP/1.1
> User-Agent: curl/7.19.7 (universal-apple-darwin10.0)
> Host: localhost:9393
> Accept: */*
>
< HTTP/1.1 200 OK
< Content-Type: text/plain;charset=utf-8
< Cache-Control: public, must-revalidate, max-age=3600
< Expires: 2011-09-26 17:35:04 -0400
< Content-Length: 48
< Server: WEBrick/1.3.1 (Ruby/1.9.2/2011-07-09)
< Date: Mon, 26 Sep 2011 20:35:04 GMT
< Connection: Keep-Alive
<
* Connection #0 to host localhost left intact
* Closing connection #0
This page rendered at 2011-09-26 16:35:04 -0400.
```

Settings Headers via expires

Sinatra has a convenient shortcut for defining cache control and content expiration that wraps up the behavior described above in a shorter method call. Specifically, you can set the appropriate headers using the `expires` helper as shown in Example 2-30.

You can use the `cache_control` helper if you only want to set the `Cache-Control` header.

Example 2-30. Setting content expiration using expires

```
require 'sinatra'

before do
  content_type :txt
end

get '/cache' do
  expires 3600, :public, :must_revalidate
  "This page rendered at #{Time.now}."
end
```

This will produce the same effect as Example 2-29.

A good resource for understanding the various caching options available via HTTP can be found at *http://www.mnot.net/cache_docs/*.

ETags

ETags, short for *entity tags*, are another way to represent how fresh a resource is via HTTP. They are server-generated identifiers that are used to "fingerprint" a resource in a given state. A client can safely assume that if the ETag for a resource has changed, then the resource itself has changed and should be fetched from the server again.

 There's no special significance to the ETag value itself; it could be a globally-unique identifier (GUID), a checksum, etc. There is no meaning attached to the particular value.

Generating ETags

ETags are nothing more than HTTP headers with values crafted by the server for consumption by clients. As such, you could use the `headers` helper to set them (as demonstrated by previous examples). There is a built-in helper specifically for ETags called, conveniently enough, `etag`. Example 2-31 demonstrates generating an ETag.

Example 2-31. Generating an ETag

```
require 'sinatra'
require 'uuid'

before do
  content_type :txt
  @guid = UUID.new.generate
end

get '/etag' do
  etag @guid
  "This resource has an ETag value of #{@guid}."
end
```

A request to this resource is now associated with a specific ETag value, which can be compared on demand to the value returned by the server to determine if anything has changed.

```
$ curl -v http://localhost:9393/etag
* About to connect() to localhost port 9393 (#0)
*   Trying 127.0.0.1... connected
* Connected to localhost (127.0.0.1) port 9393 (#0)
> GET /etag HTTP/1.1
> User-Agent: curl/7.19.7 (universal-apple-darwin10.0)
> Host: localhost:9393
> Accept: */*
>
< HTTP/1.1 200 OK
< Content-Type: text/plain;charset=utf-8
< Etag: "448c1ee0-cab2-012e-0f5e-482a14372ddf"
< Content-Length: 72
< Server: WEBrick/1.3.1 (Ruby/1.9.2/2011-07-09)
```

```
< Date: Mon, 26 Sep 2011 21:13:13 GMT
< Connection: Keep-Alive
<
* Connection #0 to host localhost left intact
* Closing connection #0
This resource has an ETag value of 448c1ee0-cab2-012e-0f5e-482a14372ddf.
```

Weak ETags

Normal ETags are considered to be *strongly-validating*; two identical ETags can be considered to refer to byte-for-byte identical resources. There is an alternative, the weak ETag, that is *weakly-validating*. Weak ETags are used to denote that resources can be considered identical or equivalent even if they are not byte-for-byte identical.

Weak ETags can be generated by passing the symbol :weak to the etag helper, as shown in Example 2-32.

Example 2-32. Generating a weak ETag

```
require 'sinatra'
require 'uuid'

before do
  content_type :txt
  @guid = UUID.new.generate
end

get '/etag' do
  etag @guid, :weak
  "This resource has an ETag value of #{@guid}."
end
```

Examining the response headers, we can see that the ETag value is prepended by "W/" to denote that the ETag is weak.

```
$ curl -v http://localhost:9393/etag
* About to connect() to localhost port 9393 (#0)
*    Trying 127.0.0.1... connected
* Connected to localhost (127.0.0.1) port 9393 (#0)
> GET /etag HTTP/1.1
> User-Agent: curl/7.19.7 (universal-apple-darwin10.0)
> Host: localhost:9393
> Accept: */*
>
< HTTP/1.1 200 OK
< Content-Type: text/plain;charset=utf-8
< Etag: W/"448c1ee0-cab2-012e-0f5e-482a14372ddf"
< Content-Length: 72
< Server: WEBrick/1.3.1 (Ruby/1.9.2/2011-07-09)
< Date: Mon, 26 Sep 2011 21:13:13 GMT
< Connection: Keep-Alive
<
* Connection #0 to host localhost left intact
```

```
* Closing connection #0
This resource has an ETag value of 448c1ee0-cab2-012e-0f5e-482a14372ddf.
```

 The server will send the ETag header, but the client will send If-None-Match to the server to validate the ETag. If you want to check ETag values from the client in your application code, look for If-None-Match.

Sessions

Although HTTP is itself a stateless protocol, one way to maintain the state for a user is through the use of *cookie-based sessions*, demonstrated in Example 2-33. In this approach, a cookie (in this case, one named `rack.session`) is stored client-side and used to house data related to the activity in the current user's session.

 A more thorough discussion of cookies in general is up next.

You can enable sessions via the `configure` block. Once enabled, the `session` object can be used to store and retrieve values.

Example 2-33. Using cookie-based session management

```
require 'sinatra'

configure do
  enable :sessions
end

before do
  content_type :txt
end

get '/set' do
  session[:foo] = Time.now
  "Session value set."
end

get '/fetch' do
  "Session value: #{session[:foo]}"
end
```

It wouldn't be very secure if we could just decode any Sinatra session out there. For the sake of security, Sinatra creates a *secret key* for you each time the application is started and uses this to protect the session state data.

There are a number of reasons you might want to set this key manually; for example, you may want to operate multiple application instances behind a load-balancer and therefore need to be able to decode session state properly on discrete servers. To set the secret key, you can do so in a `configure` block via `set :session_secret, 'your_cus tom_value_here'`.

 One caveat with cookie-based sessions: any data you store in the session collection is serialized and stored on the client. It's important to be mindful of network traffic and performance with this approach, especially if you're used to other session storage approaches where only a unique key is stored client-side (with the actual session data stored in memory on the server).

Destroying a Session

If you'd like to destroy a session, you can call `session.clear` in your routes to immediately wipe out that user's session. See Example 2-34.

Example 2-34. Destroying a session using session.clear

```
require 'sinatra'

configure do
  enable :sessions
end

before do
  content_type :txt
end

get '/set' do
  session[:foo] = Time.now
  "Session value set."
end

get '/fetch' do
  "Session value: #{session[:foo]}"
end

get '/logout' do
  session.clear
  redirect '/fetch'
end
```

Cookies

Cookies are small amounts of metadata stored client-side. There are essentially two types of cookies: *session* and *persistent*. They differ by the points at which they expire; session cookies are destroyed when the user closes his browser (or otherwise ends his session), and persistent cookies expire at a predetermined time that is stored with the cookie itself.

Although it's easy to think of cookies as being "set" server-side, the server is actually simply asking the client to take the contents of the Set-Cookie header from the response and persist it for some length of time. The client can, at its discretion, opt to send the data back to the server on subsequent requests.

Setting a cookie, in simplest form, is accomplished by calling response.set_cookie and providing a name and value as parameters; deleting is accomplished in similar fashion using repsonse.delete_cookie. Reading a cookie involves accessing the request.cook ies collection by name. See Example 2-35 for more on working with cookies.

Example 2-35. Working with cookies

```
require 'sinatra'

get '/' do
  response.set_cookie "foo", "bar"
  "Cookie set. Would you like to <a href='/read'>read it</a>?"
end

get '/read' do
  "Cookie has a value of: #{request.cookies['foo']}."
end

get '/delete' do
  response.delete_cookie "foo"
  "Cookie has been deleted."
end
```

 There are a number of optional settings for cookies, including the domain and path that the cookie can be set for. By default, clients typically set cookie paths relative to the requesting URL if none is explicitly provided. If, for example, your route were:

```
get('/set') { response.set_cookie "foo", "bar" }
```

then the cookie foo would not be sent to the server on requests to:

```
get('/read') { ... }
```

To set any of the additional options explicitly, you can pass a hash containing your settings as the second parameter:

```
response.set_cookie("foo", :value => "bar", :path => '/')
```

Attachments

As demonstrated in Example 2-36, sending attachments to clients is extremely easy in Sinatra; there is a built-in attachment method that optionally takes a filename parameter. If the filename has an extension (.jpg, .txt, etc.), that extension will be used to determine the `Content-Type` header for the response. The evaluation of the route will provide the contents of the attachment.

Example 2-36. Sending an attachment to a client

```
require 'sinatra'

before do
  content_type :txt
end

get '/attachment' do
  attachment 'name_your_attachment.txt'
  "Here's what will be sent downstream, in an attachment called 'name_your_attachment.txt'."
end
```

As always, we'll take a look at the output via cURL. You'll note the addition of the `Content-Disposition` header, which denotes both the fact that it contains an attachment and the optional filename parameter.

```
$ curl -v http://localhost:4567/attachment
* About to connect() to localhost port 4567 (#0)
*   Trying 127.0.0.1... connected
* Connected to localhost (127.0.0.1) port 4567 (#0)
> GET /attachment HTTP/1.1
> User-Agent: curl/7.19.7 (universal-apple-darwin10.0)
> Host: localhost:4567
> Accept: */*
>
< HTTP/1.1 200 OK
< X-Frame-Options: sameorigin
< X-XSS-Protection: 1; mode=block
< Content-Type: text/plain;charset=utf-8
< Content-Disposition: attachment; filename="name_your_attachment.txt"
< Content-Length: 88
< Connection: keep-alive
< Server: thin 1.2.11 codename Bat-Shit Crazy
<
* Connection #0 to host localhost left intact
* Closing connection #0
Here's what will be sent downstream, in an attachment called
'name_your_attachment.txt'.
```

Streaming

One of the most exciting new features in Sinatra (version 1.3.0 and up) is support for content streaming from your application. The streaming support abstracts away the differences in different Rack-compatible servers, leaving you to focus solely on developing the functionality you desire as opposed to the plumbing that makes it possible.

Keeping the Connection Open

There are a number of applications that lend themselves to a persistent, open connection. Perhaps you're developing a chat program or something similar; Example 2-37 shows how to create this type of connection and broadcast messages to subscribers.

Example 2-37. A simple streaming example

```ruby
require 'sinatra'

before do
  content_type :txt
end

connections = []

get '/consume' do
  stream(:keep_open) do |out|
    # store connection for later on
    connections << out

    # remove connection when closed properly
    out.callback { connections.delete(out) }

    # remove connection when closed due to an error
    out.errback do
      logger.warn 'we just lost a connection!'
      connections.delete(out)
    end
  end
end

get '/broadcast/:message' do
  connections.each do |out|
    out << "#{Time.now} -> #{params[:message]}" << "\n"
  end

  "Sent #{params[:message]} to all clients."
end
```

It's a little tricky to demonstrate the behavior in text, but a good demonstration would be to start the application, then open a web browser and navigate to *http://localhost: 4567/consume*. Next, open a terminal and use cURL to send messages to the server.

```
$ curl http://localhost:4567/broadcast/hello
Sent hello to all clients.
```

If you look back at the web browser, you should see that the content of the page has been updated with a time stamp and the message that you sent via the terminal. The connection remains open, and the client continues to wait for further information from the server.

Finite Streaming

An alternative to the long-running open connection is to simply keep it open long enough to stream some finite amount of information down to the client; this approach is shown in Example 2-38.

Example 2-38. Streaming a finite amount of information

```
require 'sinatra'

before do
  content_type :txt
end

get '/har-har' do
  stream do |out|
    out << "Wanna hear a joke about potassium?\n"
    sleep 1.5
    out << "K.\n"
    sleep 1.5
    out << "I also have one about sodium!\n"
    sleep 1.5
    out << "Na.\n"
  end
end
```

Open up a web browser or cURL, make a request to *http://localhost:4567/har-har* and enjoy!

 We've also got some great ones about photons and how on vacation they're always "traveling light."

Summary

This chapter covered the bulk of Sinatra fundamentals: the HTTP verbs, defining routes, halting and redirecting routes, delivering static resources, using filters, and the configuration block. Next, we'll discuss Sinatra from a much lower level and explore how it really works so that we can make full use of the advanced features it provides.

## CHAPTER 3

A Peek Behind the Curtain

At this point you should be feeling fairly comfortable writing Sinatra applications. So far, we've focused primarily on the classic approach, where a single application exists in a single process. That's only scratching the surface of Sinatra's potential, however. Let's take a deeper look at how Sinatra actually works. Once you understand what is going on backstage, it becomes significantly easier to take full advantage of the available API (or even extend it). To gain this understanding, we'll dig into the source code and take a guided tour of what's actually going on.

Sinatra follows Semantic Versioning, which basically states that Sinatra will not break backwards compatibility unless the major version (the first number of the version) is increased. So, any application written for Sinatra 1.2.3 will still work with Sinatra 1.3.0. Semantic Versioning requires an official and complete API specification. For Sinatra, this happens to be the *README*, which you can find here: *http://www.sinatrarb .com/intro*. You can learn more about Semantic Versioning at *http:// semver.org/*.

Application and Delegation

Let's start with a quick experiment. We saw earlier in the book how parameters are passed into routes and extracted in the context of the route via the `params` hash; for example, in a simple login form we may find `params[:username]` and `params[:password]`.

We mentioned previously that the various route definitions in a Sinatra app (`get '/ home'`, `post '/login'`, etc.) are not themselves method definitions, but rather calls to methods deeper in Sinatra. The behavior your route should take is passed as a block (or *closure*) for Sinatra to handle and execute.

This gets interesting when examining the context in which the block is executed. A block in Ruby is supposed to have the same methods and variables that the defining scope has. So, what would you expect to see as output from the code in Example 3-1?

Example 3-1. A simple script to check the availability of params

```
$ irb
ruby-1.9.2-p0 > require 'sinatra'
 => true
ruby-1.9.2-p0 > get('/') { defined? params }
 => [/^\/$/, [], [], #>Proc:0x00000100aff310@/sinatra-1.2.6/lib/sinatra/base.rb:1152>]
ruby-1.9.2-p0 > defined? params
 => nil
```

As it turns out, `params` is available only inside the scope of the get block. The secret to Sinatra's magic is how it handles management of `self`.

The Inner Self

In Ruby, method calls that aren't sent to a variable or constant are actually sent to `self`; typically `self` is omitted for brevity. Take a look at Example 3-2, where we call `jobs` and `self.jobs`; the output is the same because both calls are made in the same scope and the identity of `self` is identical.

Example 3-2. Demonstrating the optional use of self

```
$ irb
ruby-1.9.2-p0 > jobs
 => #0->irb on main (#<Thread:0x00000100887678>: running)
ruby-1.9.2-p0 > self.jobs
 => #0->irb on main (#<Thread:0x00000100887678>: running)
```

The identity of `self` becomes important when crossing what are known as *scope gates*; scope gates are sections of code where the context of the executing code changes, and generally `self` changes accordingly. In Ruby, class definitions, module definitions, and methods are all scope gates.

Example 3-3 shows the results when `self` is inspected inside and outside of a Sinatra route; see Figure 3-1 for the rendered output.

Example 3-3. Inspecting self in different scopes

```
require "sinatra"

outer_self = self
get '/' do
  content_type :txt
  "outer self: #{outer_self}, inner self: #{self}"
end
```

Technically speaking, closures in Ruby open a new, nested scope. We'll see more on this in a moment.

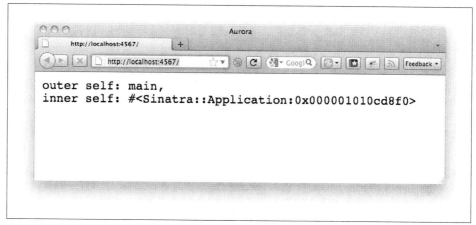

Figure 3-1. Examining the state of self in different scopes

What Example 3-3 tells us is that all method calls in the routing blocks are actually sent to an instance of the class `Sinatra::Application`. Furthermore, if you refresh the page, take note of the object id; it changes on each refresh, indicating that there is a separate instance for every request made.

 It's also worth noting that the outer scope is `main`, the same as it was when calling `jobs` and `self.jobs` in the IRB session.

Where Does get Come From?

So we know now that our routes are passing blocks to instances of `Sinatra::Applica` `tion` for evaluation. Where exactly do these route methods live? Let's open IRB and work with the Ruby reflection API to get a general idea of the class structure as demonstrated in Example 3-4.

Example 3-4. Using reflection in IRB

```
[~]$ irb
ruby-1.9.2-p180 > require 'sinatra'
 => true
ruby-1.9.2-p180 > Sinatra::Application.superclass
 => Sinatra::Base
ruby-1.9.2-p180 > Sinatra::Base.superclass
 => Object
ruby-1.9.2-p180 > method(:get)
 => #<Method: Object(Sinatra::Delegator)#get>
ruby-1.9.2-p180 > Sinatra::Delegator.methods(false)
 => [:delegate, :target, :target=]
ruby-1.9.2-p180 > Sinatra::Delegator.target
 => Sinatra::Application
ruby-1.9.2-p180 > Sinatra::Application.method(:get)
```

```
 => #<Method: Sinatra::Application(Sinatra::Base).get>
ruby-1.9.2-p180 > _.source_location
 => ["~/gems/sinatra-1.3.0/lib/sinatra/base.rb", 1069]
```

Now that's interesting. Methods like get, post, and so on are actually defined *twice*. One definition is made in Sinatra::Delegator, which is a mixin extending Object. Those methods are therefore available everywhere in the application. The delegator mixin will simply send the same method call to Sinatra::Application, which inherits them from Sinatra::Base.

 Mixins are a technique Ruby inherited from Common Lisp, which allows you to not only choose a superclass but also to add other class-like objects to the inheritance chain. This enables you to extend already existing classes and objects without overriding other methods accidentally.

Let's play with Sinatra::Base and Sinatra::Application a bit more to get a better sense of where features are made available. Example 3-5 shows how to properly define route handlers without using the DSL, and what happens if you try to define them on the wrong module.

Example 3-5. Using reflection in IRB, continued

```
[~]$ irb
ruby-1.9.2-p180 > require 'sinatra/base'
 => true
ruby-1.9.2-p180 > get('/') { 'hi' }
NoMethodError: undefined method `get' for main:Object
  from (irb):3
ruby-1.9.2-p180 > Sinatra::Application.get('/') { 'hi' }
 => []
ruby-1.9.2-p180 > Sinatra::Application.run!
== Sinatra/1.3.0 has taken the stage on 4567 for development with backup from Thin
>> Thin web server (v1.2.11 codename Bat-Shit Crazy)
>> Maximum connections set to 1024
>> Listening on 0.0.0.0:4567, CTRL+C to stop
```

Exploring the Implementation

Although we've used the top-level DSL thus far in the book, Sinatra is still perfectly usable without it, requiring only *sinatra/base* and a little knowledge of the mixin structure to spin up an application. This means that the top-level DSL is *totally optional*.

Examples 3-4 and 3-5 show that the source for *base.rb* contained the definition for the get method (and indeed is the heart of Sinatra as a whole). Close to the end of the file, you'll find the implementations of both the Application class and the Delegator mixin. The implementation is surprisingly simple (don't be too distracted by the register method; it's simply to ensure that methods added by extensions, like *sinatra-name-*

---

space, are available from the top-level DSL as well). All the heavy lifting in Sinatra's execution takes place in the **Base** class.

The current development version of *base.rb* can be found at *https://github.com/sinatra/sinatra/blob/master/lib/sinatra/base.rb*. Replace *master* with any version (i.e. *1.3.0*) to take a look at the file that shipped with it. If you see the content displayed in Figure 3-2, you've come to the right place.

Figure 3-2. Exploring Sinatra's source on GitHub

Helpers and Extensions

Now we've armed ourselves with enough knowledge to be a little dangerous with Sinatra. We know now that we don't have to rely on the DSL, but can engage Sinatra in a completely *modular* fashion. This begs the question of what we stand to gain by doing so. After all, the DSL is capable and convenient out of the box. What if, however, we want to do something that Sinatra's DSL doesn't natively allow?

There are two primary ways to extend Sinatra's functionality: *extension methods* and *helpers*. You've used extension methods already; an example would be the route handlers (such as `get`) that make up the average classic application. Usually used at application load time, extension methods are mostly used for configuration and routing, and map directly to class methods for `Sinatra::Base` or subclasses. It's the responsibility of `Sinatra::Base` to make sure everything works properly.

 When creating extension and helper methods, it's considered a best practice to wrap those in a module and use the `register` method to let Sinatra figure out where to use those modules as mixins. Be kind to your fellow Sinatra developers!

Creating Sinatra Extensions

Let's take a moment to create a simple extension to Sinatra. Our fictional application for this example requires us to send both GET and POST requests to a particular URL such that the same block of code handles both verbs. We're Ruby developers, so we try to keep our code DRY and we obviously don't want to define two routes with identical code. Therefore, it makes sense to define an extension that can handle our requirement without duplication. A simple extension is shown in Example 3-6.

Example 3-6. Creating the Sinatra::PostGet extension

```ruby
require 'sinatra/base'

module Sinatra
  module PostGet
    def post_get(route, &block)
      get(route, &block)
      post(route, &block)
    end
  end

  # now we just need to register it via Sinatra::Base
  register PostGet
end
```

Go ahead and create a quick Sinatra app and a module extension in a "sinatra" subfolder; your file should be called *post_get.rb*. Example 3-7 shows how to actually make use of your new extension.

 Once you've tried the extension and observed it functioning, try removing the `register PostGet` call from the module. What happens?

Example 3-7. Using custom Sinatra::PostGet extension

```
require 'sinatra'
require './sinatra/post_get'

post_get '/' do
  "Hi #{params[:name]}"
end
```

Now we can crack open Telnet again and try our multiple route handler.

```
$ telnet 0.0.0.0 4567
Trying 0.0.0.0...
Connected to 0.0.0.0.
Escape character is '^]'.
GET / HTTP/1.1
Host: 0.0.0.0

  HTTP/1.1 200 OK
  Content-Type: text/html;charset=utf-8
  Content-Length: 3
  Connection: keep-alive
  Server: thin 1.2.11 codename Bat-Shit Crazy

  Hi

POST / HTTP/1.1
Host: localhost:4567
Content-Length: 7

foo=bar

  HTTP/1.1 200 OK
  Content-Type: text/html;charset=utf-8
  Content-Length: 3
  Connection: keep-alive
  Server: thin 1.2.11 codename Bat-Shit Crazy

  Hi
```

Success! We now have a custom extension that allows us to respond to two verbs in one route without duplicating any code. The extension approach excels at handling low-level routing and configuration requirements deftly.

Helpers

Helpers and extensions are something like cousins: you can recognize them both as being from the same family, but they have quite different roles to play. Instead of calling `register` to let Sinatra know about them, you pass them to `helpers`. Most importantly, they're available both in the block you pass to your route and the view template itself, making them effective across application tiers.

Let's look at an archetypical helper method: one that generates hyperlinks. The code is shown in Example 3-8.

Example 3-8. A helper method that generates hyperlinks

```
require 'sinatra/base'

module Sinatra
  module LinkHelper
    def link(name)
      case name
      when :about then '/about'
      when :index then '/index'
      else "/page/#{name}"
      end
    end
  end

  helpers LinkHelper
end
```

All you need to do is `require './sinatra/link_helper'` in your main Sinatra application, and you'll be able to make use of the `LinkHelper` module throughout. Let's make a quick view in Erb that tests it, demonstrated in Example 3-9.

Example 3-9. An Erb view to test the module

```
<html>
<head>
  <title>Link Helper Test</title>
</head>
<body>
  <nav>
    <ul>
      <li><a href="<%= link(:index) %>">Index</a></li>
      <li><a href="<%= link(:about) %>">About</a></li>
      <li><a href="<%= link(:random) %>">Random</a></li>
    </ul>
  </nav>
</body>
</html>
```

Our links are nicely rendered, and mousing over indicates they're pointing to */index*, */about*, and */page/random* as intended.

Helpers Without Modules

Sometimes you need to create a helper or two that are only going to be used in one application or for a specific purpose. The `helpers` method used in Example 3-10 accommodates this case by accepting a block, avoiding the overhead of creating modules, and so on.

Example 3-10. Creating a helper via a block

```
require 'sinatra'
helpers do
  def link(name)
    case name
    when :about then '/about'
    when :index then '/index'
    else "/page/#{name}"
    end
  end
end

get '/' do
  erb :index
end

get '/index.html' do
  redirect link(:index)
end

__END__

@@index
<a href="<%= link :about %>">about</a>
```

 What's up with the funky @@index stuff at the bottom of Example 3-10? It's what Sinatra refers to as an *inline template*. Got a small amount of HTML to deliver and don't want to create a whole view file dedicated to it? You can provide it after your routing code and call it the same way you would a normal view. Figure 3-3 shows the rendered output of our friendly helpers.

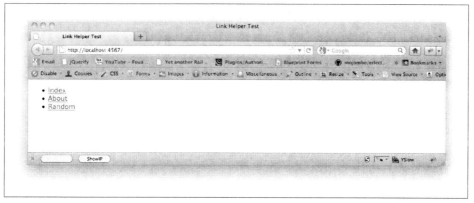

Figure 3-3. Using the link helper module

Combining Helpers and Extensions

What if you want to create an extension that ships with a helper as well? Sinatra provides a hook for this type of activity via a method called **registered**. Simply create a **regis tered** method that takes the application class as an argument. Example 3-11 provides an example of how you might organize your methods; register them with Sinatra as shown and it becomes trivial to produce some fairly sweeping changes to how Sinatra executes.

Example 3-11. Combining helpers with extensions

```
require 'sinatra/base'
module MyExtension
  module Helpers
    # helper methods go here
  end

  # extension methods go here

  def self.registered(app)
    app.helpers Helpers
  end
end

Sinatra.register MyExtension
```

Request and Response

The next step in understanding Sinatra's internals is to examine the flow of a request, from parsing to delivery of a response back to the client. To do so, we need to examine the role of *Rack* (which we've mentioned briefly earlier) in the Sinatra landscape.

Rack

Rack is a specification implemented by not only Sinatra, but also Rails, Merb, Ramaze, and a number of other Ruby projects. It's an extremely simple protocol specifying how an HTTP server (such as Thin, which we've used throughout the book) interfaces with an application object, like **Sinatra::Application**, without having to know anything about Sinatra in particular. In short, Rack defines the higher-level vocabulary that hardware and software can use to communicate. The Rack homepage, *http://rack.ru byforge.org*, is shown in Figure 3-4.

The Rack protocol at its core specifies that the application object, the so-called *endpoint*, has to respond to the method call. The server, usually referred to as the *handler*, will call that method with one parameter. This parameter is a hash containing all relevant information about the request: this includes the HTTP verb used by the request, the path that is requested, the headers that have been sent by the client, and so on.

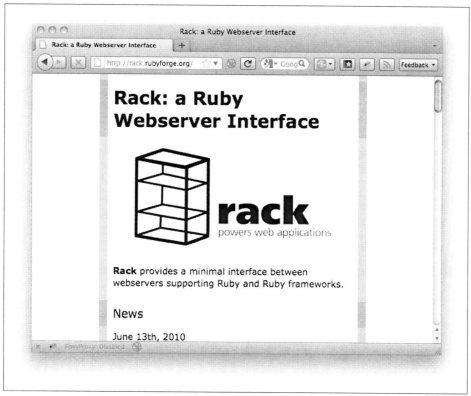

Figure 3-4. You can learn more about Rack at http://rack.rubyforge.org

The method is expected to return an array with three elements. The first one is the status code, provided as an integer. For example, a successful request may receive status code 200, indicating that no errors occurred. The second element is a hash (or hash-like object in Rack 1.3 or later) containing all the response headers. Here you'll find information such as whether or not the client should cache the response, the length of the response, and similar information. The last object is the *body* object. This object is required to behave like an array of strings; that is, it has to respond to each and call the passed block with strings.

Sinatra Without Sinatra

What's neat about this is that it's completely possible (and acceptable) to run a Sinatra application without truly invoking Sinatra. Let's try to port a simple Sinatra application to pure Rack, shown in Example 3-12.

Example 3-12. Simplified equivalent of a Sinatra application using Rack

```
module MySinatra
  class Application
```

```
    def self.call(env)
      new.call(env)
    end

    def call(env)
      headers = {'Content-Type' => 'text/html'}
      if env['PATH_INFO'] == '/'
        status, body = 200, 'hi'
      else
        status, body = 404, "Sinatra doesn't know this ditty!"
      end
      headers['Content-Length'] = body.length.to_s
      [status, headers, [body]]
    end
  end
end

require 'thin'
Thin::Server.start MySinatra::Application, 4567
```

Example 3-12 is roughly equivalent to get('/') { 'hi' }. Of course, this is not the implementation found in Sinatra, since the Sinatra implementation is generic and handles a larger number of use cases, contains wrappers, optimizations, and so on. Sinatra will, however, wrap the env hash in a convenience object, available to your code in the form of the request object. Likewise, response is available for generating the body array. These are easily accessible in your application; take a look at Example 3-13 to see how they're used.

Example 3-13. Using env, request, and response in Sinatra

```
require 'sinatra'

helpers do
  def assert(condition)
    fail "something is terribly broken" unless condition
  end
end

get '/' do
  assert env['PATH_INFO'] == request.path_info

  final_result = response.finish
  assert Array === final_result
  assert final_result.length == 3
  assert final_result.first == 200

  "everything is fine"
end
```

Rack It Up

What does all this mean for us as Sinatra developers? If you hop into IRB again and try typing `Sinatra::Application.new.class`, you will find that `new` does not return an instance of `Sinatra::Application` (give it a shot; it actually returns an instance of `Rack::MethodOverride`).

The Rack specification supports chaining filters and routers in front of your application. In Rack slang, those are called *middleware*. This middleware also implements the Rack specification; it responds to `call` and returns an array as described above. Instead of simply creating that array on its own, it will use different Rack endpoint or middleware and simply call `call` on that object. Now this middleware can modify the request (the `env` hash), modify the response, decide whether or not to call the next endpoint, or any combination of those. By returning a `Rack::MethodOverride` object instead of a `Sinatra::Application` object, Sinatra respects this middleware chaining.

Middleware

Rack has an additional specification for middleware. Middleware is created by a *factory* object. This object has to respond to *new*; *new* takes at least one argument, which is the endpoint that will be wrapped by the middleware. Finally, the middleware returns the wrapped endpoint.

Usually the factory is simply a class, like `Sinatra::ShowException`, and the instances of this class are the concrete middleware configurations, with a fixed endpoint. Let's set Sinatra aside for a moment and write a simple Rack application again. We can use a `Proc` object for that, since it responds to `call`. We will also create a simple middleware that will check if the path is correct.

The `rack` gem should already be installed on your system, since Sinatra depends on it. It comes with a handy tool called *rackup*, which understands a simple DSL for setting up a Rack application (you may recall we used a rackup file in Chapter 1 to deploy code to Heroku). Create a file called *config.ru* with the contents shown in Example 3-14. Once you've done so, run **rackup -p 4567 -s thin** from the same directory. You should be able to view your application at *http://localhost:4567/*.

Example 3-14. Contents of config.ru

```
MyApp = proc do |env|
  [200, {'Content-Type' => 'text/plain'}, ['ok']]
end

class MyMiddleware
  def initialize(app)
    @app = app
  end

  def call(env)
```

```
    if env['PATH_INFO'] == '/'
      @app.call(env)
    else
      [404, {'Content-Type' => 'text/plain'}, ['not ok']]
    end
  end
end

# this is the actual configuration
use MyMiddleware
run MyApp
```

Sinatra and Middleware

The features exposed by Rack are so handy that Sinatra actually ships with a use method that behaves exactly like the version offered by *rackup*. Example 3-15 shows it in use.

Example 3-15. Using use in Sinatra

```
require 'sinatra'
require 'rack'

# A handy middleware that ships with Rack
# and sets the X-Runtime header
use Rack::Runtime

get('/') { 'Hello world!' }
```

Although interesting, the question lingers: how does this all connect to day-to-day development in Sinatra? The answer: you can use *any* Sinatra application as middleware.

The class, Sinatra::Application, is the factory creating the configured middleware instance (which is your application instance). When the request comes in, all *before filters* are triggered. Then, if a route matches, the corresponding block will be executed. If no route matches, the request is handed off to the wrapped application. The *after filters* are executed after we've got a response back from the route or wrapped app. Thus, your application is Rack middleware.

Dispatching

There is, however, one catch: Sinatra relies on the "one instance per request" principle. However, when running as middleware, all requests will use the same instance over and over again. Sinatra performs a clever trick here: instead of executing the logic right away, it duplicates the current instance and hands responsibility on to the *duplicate* instead. Since instance creation (especially with all the middleware being set up internally) is not free from a performance and resources standpoint, it uses that trick for all requests (even if running as endpoint) by keeping a *prototype* object around.

Example 3-16 shows the secret sauce in Sinatra's dispatch activities.

Example 3-16. The Sinatra dispatch in action

```
module MySinatra
  class Base
    def self.prototype
      @prototype ||= new
    end

    def self.call(env)
      prototype.call(env)
    end

    def call(env)
      dup.call!(env)
    end

    def call!(env)
      [200, {'Content-Type' => 'text/plain'},
        ['routing logic not implemented']]
    end
  end

  class Application < Base
  end
end
```

Dispatching Redux

This lets us craft some pretty interesting Sinatra applications. This prototype and instance duplication approach means you can safely use `call` on the current instance and
consume the result of another route. If you remember from the earlier discussion on
Rack's methodology, the `call` method will return an array. The application in Example 3-17 lets you check the status code and headers of other routes. Figure 3-5 shows
the output of the inspector application.

Example 3-17. A reflective route inspector

```
require 'sinatra'

get '/example' do
  'go to /inspect/example'
end

get '/inspect/*' do
  route  = "/" + params[:splat].first
  data   = call env.merge("PATH_INFO" => route)
  result = "Status: #{data[0]}\n"

  data[1].each do |header, value|
    result << "#{header}: #{value}\n"
  end
```

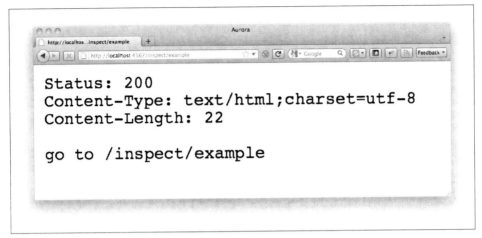

Figure 3-5. Firing another request internally to inspect the response

```
    result << "\n"
    data[2].each do |line|
      result << line
    end

    content_type :txt
    result
end
```

Now let's tie everything together with the code in Example 3-18 and create a Sinatra application that acts as middleware.

Example 3-18. Using Sinatra as middleware in a fictional Rails project

```
require './sinatra_middleware'
require './config/environment'

use Sinatra::Application
run MyRailsProject::Application
```

Changing Bindings

To bring the discussion back to where we began, let's focus on a block passed to *get* again. How is it that the instance methods are actually available? If you've been working with Ruby for a decent length of time, you've probably come across `instance_eval`, which allows you to dynamically change the binding of a block. Example 3-19 demonstrates how this can be used.

Example 3-19. Toying with instance_eval

```
$ irb
ruby-1.9.2-p180 > array = ['foo', 'bar']
```

```
      1084    private¬
      1085        def route(verb, path, options={}, &block)¬
      1086            # Because of self.options.host¬
      1087            host_name(options.delete(:host)) if options.key?(:host)¬
      1088            enable :empty_path_info if path == "" and empty_path_info.nil?¬
      1089            (@routes[verb] ||= []) << compile!(verb, path, block, options)¬
      1090            invoke_hook(:route_added, verb, path, block)¬
      1091        end¬
      1092    ¬
      1093        def invoke_hook(name, *args)¬
      1094            extensions.each { |e| e.send(name, *args) if e.respond_to?(name) }¬
      1095        end¬
      1096    ¬
      1097        def generate_method(method_name, &block)¬
      1098            define_method(method_name, &block)¬
      1099            method = instance_method method_name¬
      1100            remove_method method_name¬
      1101            method¬
      1102        end¬
      1103    ¬
      1104        def compile!(verb, path, block, options = {})¬
      1105            options.each_pair { |option, args| send(option, *args) }¬
      1106            method_name          = "#{verb} #{path}"¬
      1107            unbound_method       = generate_method(method_name, &block)¬
      1108            pattern, keys        = compile path¬
      1109            conditions, @conditions = @conditions, []¬
      1110    ¬
      1111            [ pattern, keys, conditions, block.arity != 0 ?¬
      1112                proc { |a,p| unbound_method.bind(a).call(*p) } :¬
      1113                proc { |a,p| unbound_method.bind(a).call } ]¬
      1114        end¬
      1115    ¬
      1116        def compile(path)¬
      1117            keys = []¬
```

Line: 1113 Column: 53   ◉ Ruby   ‡ ◉ ▼ Soft Tabs: 2 ‡   compile!(verb, path, block, options = {})   ‡

Figure 3-6. generate_method and its usage in Sinatra

```
 => ['foo', 'bar']
ruby-1.9.2-p180 > block = proc { first }
 => #<Proc:0x00000101017c58@(irb):2>
ruby-1.9.2-p180 > block.call
NameError: undefined local variable or method `first' for main:Object
  from (irb):2:in `block in irb_binding'
  from (irb):3:in `call'
  from (irb):3
  from /Users/konstantin/.rvm/rubies/ruby-1.9.2-p180/bin/irb:16:in `<main>'
ruby-1.9.2-p180 > array.instance_eval(&block)
 => "foo"
```

This is similar to what Sinatra does. In fact, earlier versions of Sinatra do use `instance_eval`. However, there is an alternative: dynamically create a method from that block, get the *unbound method object* for that method, and remove the method immediately. When you want to run the code, bind the method object to the current instance and call it.

This has a few advantages over `instance_eval`: it results in significantly better performance since the scope change only occurs once as opposed to every request. It also allows the passing of arguments to the block. Moreover, since you can name the method yourself, it results in more readable stack traces. All of this logic is wrapped in Sinatra's `generate_method`, which you can examine in Figure 3-6 and Example 3-20.

 `generate_method` is used internally by Sinatra and is not part of the public API. You should not use it directly in your application.

Example 3-20. generate_method from sinatra/base.rb

```
def generate_method(method_name, &block)
  define_method(method_name, &block)
  method = instance_method method_name
  remove_method method_name
  method
end
```

Summary

This has been a deep chapter! It's certainly a lot to take in given how simple and straightforward Sinatra is on the surface. We have started by digging just a little deeper into Sinatra's implementation details with every step in this chapter. By now, you should have a general understanding of what is going on, how the routing system works, and what Sinatra will do with the results.

We also introduced you to Rack in this chapter, which is the foundation for basically any and all Ruby web applications you're likely to run across. Understanding Rack will also help you understand the internals of other Ruby web frameworks and libraries (such as Rails) or web servers (like Thin). Understanding how Sinatra and Rack tick will help us design cleaner and more powerful applications, and opens the doors from a creative architecture standpoint.

In Chapter 4, we will have a look into *modular applications*, which allows Sinatra to be an even better Rack citizen.

## CHAPTER 4

Modular Applications

In Chapter 3, we saw that normal Sinatra applications actually live in `Sinatra::Appli cation`, which is a subclass of `Sinatra::Base`. Apparently, if we don't use the Top Level DSL, it is possible to just `require 'sinatra/base'`. And it shouldn't be surprising by now that it is common practice to actually do so. If we do, we usually don't use `Sina tra::Application`, but instead we create our own subclass of `Sinatra::Base`.

This style is called a *modular application*, as opposed to *classic applications* that are using the Top Level DSL. While classic applications assume a certain style by default and extend `Object`, starting with a modular application assumes next to nothing about your application setup.

 For some reason, it is a common misconception that modular applications are superior to classic applications, and that really advanced users only use modular style. From time to time it has even been proposed to drop classic style all together. This is utter nonsense and no one on the Sinatra core team shares this view. Sinatra is all about simplicity and if you can use a classic application, you should.

But why would one want to use modular style? If you activate the Top Level DSL (by requiring `sinatra`), Sinatra extends the Object class, somewhat polluting the global namespace. This is not as bad as it sounds, since all delegation methods are marked private, just like Ruby's built-in global methods, like `puts`. But still, especially if you ship your Sinatra application with a Gem, you might want to avoid this. Another use case is combining multiple Sinatra applications in a single process or using Sinatra as Rack middleware. You can, of course, combine a classic application with a modular one, but there can only be one classic application per Ruby process.

Sinatra actually jumps through some hoops to not break your objects in classic style. For example, if you implement a `method_missing` proxy (i.e. catch all methods with `method_missing` and delegate those calls to another object) and you implement `respond_to?` properly, the Sinatra DSL methods will not be triggered and `method_missing` will be called instead.

Subclassing Sinatra

Creating a subclass itself should not be that hard, but what about those DSL methods? In Chapter 4 we observed that method calls with an implicit receiver are actually sent to `self`. Now, inside a class body, `self` is actually the class itself. Therefore we can simply use the Sinatra DSL inside the class body. Make sure you only `require 'sinatra/base'` to avoid activating the Top Level DSL unintentionally. See Example 4-1.

Example 4-1. Creating your own Subclass

```
require "sinatra/base"

class MyApp < Sinatra::Base
  get '/' do
    "Hello from MyApp!"
  end
end
```

We could also define routes from outside that class body, as shown in Example 4-2, but that is rather uncommon.

Example 4-2. Routes outside of the class body

```
require "sinatra/base"

class MyApp < Sinatra::Base; end

MyApp.get '/' do
  "Hello from MyApp!"
end
```

Running Modular Applications

It seems easy so far, but if you save that code in a Ruby file and run it, nothing happens. If you replace `require "sinatra/base"` with `require "sinatra"` it will actually start a web server. But our route is missing. Think about it, `require "sinatra"` will start a server for `Sinatra::Application`, not for `MyApp`.

Using run!

Let's figure out what Sinatra is doing to start a server for a classic application. Taking a look at *lib/sinatra.rb*, shown in Figure 4-1, in the Sinatra repository quickly reveals

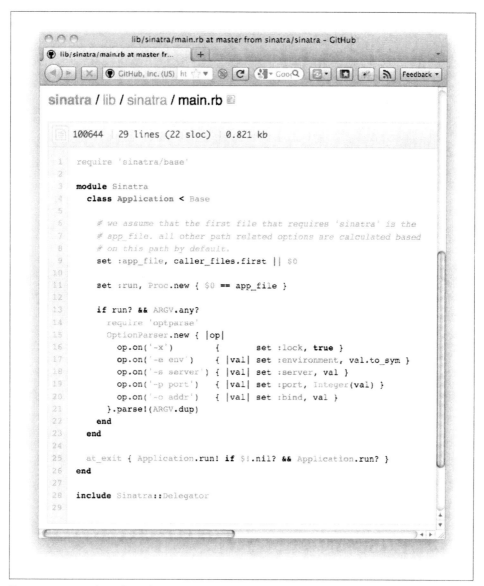

Figure 4-1. main.rb on GitHub

that all it's doing is loading *lib/sinatra/base.rb* and *lib/sinatra/main.rb*. Since the server does not start when we load *base.rb*, that logic is probably somewhere in *main.rb*.

Skimming through the code, you might notice the **at_exit** block. This is a hook offered by Ruby. Any block passed to **at_exit** will be called right before the Ruby program is going to exit. Sinatra wraps that logic there to allow us to actually define routes before starting the server. We don't really need this for our modular application. Since we are going to start the server explicitly anyway, we can simply do so after defining our routes. As you might have already guessed, run! will start a server. See Example 4-3.

Example 4-3. Serving a modular application with run!

```
require "sinatra/base"

class MyApp < Sinatra::Base
  get '/' do
    "Hello from MyApp!"
  end

  run!
end
```

Sinatra wants to make sure that the server really only starts when appropriate. Therefore it makes sure to run only if the Ruby file was executed directly and if no unhandled exception occurred. The exception handling doesn't matter for us, since we don't trigger the server from an at_exit hook. Ruby won't reach the line with run! on it if there has been an exception. We should check if the file has been executed directly, otherwise code used for testing, rackup, or anything similar won't be able to load our application. Example 4-4 demonstrates how we can make this type of check.

Example 4-4. Only start a server if the file has been executed directly

```
require "sinatra/base"

class MyApp < Sinatra::Base
  get '/' do
    "Hello from MyApp!"
  end

  # $0 is the executed file
  # __FILE__ is the current file
  run! if __FILE__ == $0
end
```

With rackup

Most deployment scenarios probably require a config.ru. We have already looked into this in Chapter 3 and it should be pretty straightforward to write and run such a configuration. Just use the code in Example 4-5 and launch the server with **rackup -s thin -p 4567**.

Example 4-5. config.ru for running a modular application

```
require "./my_app"
run MyApp
```

About Settings

Before we examine more advanced features of modular application, let's investigate *settings* for a moment. We've already used settings in Chapter 2. You can write settings at class or top level with `set :key, 'value'`. It is now possible to access those via the `settings` object.

 You can also use `enable :key` (see Example 4-6) and `disable :key`, which are syntactic sugar for `set :key, true` and `set :key, false` respectively.

Example 4-6. Reading and writing settings

```
require 'sinatra'

set :title, "My Website"

# configure let's you specify env dependent options
configure :development, :test do
  enable :admin_access
end

if settings.admin_access?
  get('/admin') { 'welcome to the admin area' }
end

get '/' do
  "<h1>#{ settings.title }</h1>"
end
```

Settings and Classes

Another short code survey reveals that `settings` is actually just an alias for the current application class. Moreover, `settings` is available both as class and as instance method as shown in Example 4-7. Figure 4-2 shows the list of default settings available to Sinatra.

Example 4-7. Definition of settings in lib/sinatra/base.rb

```
# Access settings defined with Base.set.
def self.settings
  self
end

# Access settings defined with Base.set.
def settings
  self.class.settings
end
```

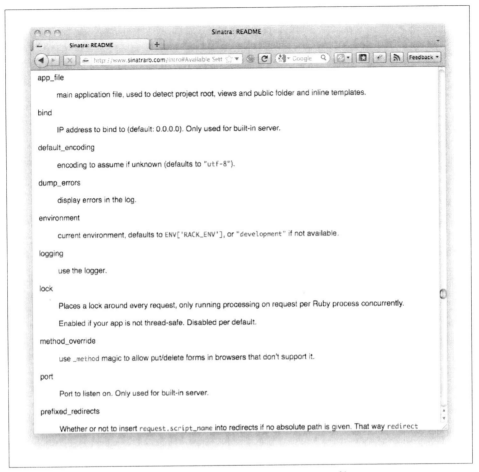

Figure 4-2. A list of default settings is available in Sinatra's README file

Without having to look at the code, it should become apparent that **set** is just some nice syntax for defining methods on the application class. In fact, **set** may also take a block instead of the value defining a method from that block; see Example 4-8 for a demonstration.

 We've already seen something similar happening to route blocks in Chapter 3. And indeed, Sinatra is using **define_method** once again, but this time to define class methods instead of instance methods.

Example 4-8. Playing with set in IRB

```
[~]$ irb
ruby-1.9.2-p180 > require 'sinatra/base'
 => true
```

```
ruby-1.9.2-p180 > class MyApp < Sinatra::Base; end
 => nil
ruby-1.9.2-p180 > MyApp.settings
 => MyApp
ruby-1.9.2-p180 > MyApp.set :foo, 42
 => MyApp
ruby-1.9.2-p180 > MyApp.foo
 => 42
ruby-1.9.2-p180 > MyApp.foo?
 => true
ruby-1.9.2-p180 > MyApp.set(:bar) { rand < 0.5 ? false : foo }
 => MyApp
ruby-1.9.2-p180 > MyApp.bar
 => false
ruby-1.9.2-p180 > MyApp.bar
 => 42
```

Subclassing Subclasses

Mapping everything to methods and embracing Ruby's object model makes Sinatra classes extremely flexible. Following the main Sinatra principle of enabling flexibility by embracing simplicity, robustness, and through-and-through clean code becomes once again visible when creating subclasses of subclasses. Since settings are directly mapped to methods, those are inherited just like normal methods, as shown in Example 4-9.

Example 4-9. Settings and inheritance

```
[~]$ irb
ruby-1.9.2-p180 > require 'sinatra/base'
 => true
ruby-1.9.2-p180 > class GeneralApp < Sinatra::Base; end
 => nil
ruby-1.9.2-p180 > class CustomApp < GeneralApp; end
 => nil
ruby-1.9.2-p180 > GeneralApp.set :foo, 42
 => MyApp
ruby-1.9.2-p180 > GeneralApp.foo
 => 42
ruby-1.9.2-p180 > CustomApp.foo
 => 42
ruby-1.9.2-p180 > CustomApp.set :foo, 23
 => 23
ruby-1.9.2-p180 > CustomApp.foo
 => 23
ruby-1.9.2-p180 > GeneralApp.foo
 => 42
```

Route Inheritance

Not only settings, but every aspect of a Sinatra class will be inherited by its subclasses. This includes defined routes, all the error handlers, extensions, middleware, and so on.

But most importantly, it will be inherited just the way methods are inherited. In case you should define a route for a class after having subclassed that class, the route will also be available in the subclass. Yet, just like methods defined in subclasses, routes in subclasses precede routes defined in the superclass, no matter when those have been defined; see Example 4-10 for a demonstration of subclassing.

Example 4-10. Inherited routes

```
require 'sinatra/base'

class GeneralApp < Sinatra::Base
  get '/about' do
    "this is a general app"
  end
end

class CustomApp < GeneralApp
  get '/about' do
    "this is a custom app"
  end
end

# This route will also be available in CustomApp
GeneralApp.get '/' do
  "<a href='/about'>more infos</a>"
end

CustomApp.run!
```

Architecture

Sinatra does not impose any application architecture on you but opens up a lot of possibilities. For instance, you can use inheritance to build a more complex controller architecture. Let's take some inspiration from Rails controllers and start with a general application controller all other controllers inherit from.

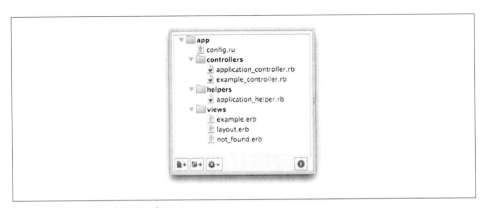

Figure 4-3. Example directory listing

Let's create a boiler plate template for a Sinatra application with a *controllers*, *helpers*, and *views* directory. If you'd add a *models* directory, you'd be ready to go for Rails-style MVC. An example directory structure can be seen in Figure 4-3.

Just like Rails, we start with an `ApplicationController` class all the other controllers can inherit from. In that controller we'll set up the *views* folder, enable logging for all environments but the `test` environment, set up a global helpers module we'll define elsewhere, and add a `not_found` handler all other controllers will inherit. Example 4-11 sets up the foundation for our class.

Example 4-11. controllers/application_controller.rb

```ruby
class ApplicationController < Sinatra::Base
  helpers ApplicationHelper

  # set folder for templates to ../views, but make the path absolute
  set :views, File.expand_path('../../views', __FILE__)

  # don't enable logging when running tests
  configure :production, :development do
    enable :logging
  end

  # will be used to display 404 error pages
  not_found do
    title 'Not Found!'
    erb :not_found
  end
end
```

You might have noticed the `title` method used in the error handler. That's not part of Sinatra, so let's implement it in the `ApplicationHelper` as shown in Example 4-12.

Example 4-12. helpers/application_helper.rb

```ruby
module ApplicationHelper
  def title(value = nil)
    @title = value if value
    @title ? "Controller Demo - #{@title}" : "Controller Demo"
  end
end
```

We can use this method to set and retrieve the current page title in both the controllers and the views. Since we have the *views* path set up properly, we can create a *layout.erb* that will be used to wrap all other ERB templates.

Example 4-13. views/layout.erb

```erb
<html>
  <head>
    <title><%= title %></title>
  </head>
  <body>
```

```
    <%= yield %>
  </body>
</html>
```

And a *not_found.rb* used for 404 error pages.

Example 4-14. views/not_fosvund.erb

```
Page does not exist! Check out the <a href='/example'>example page</a>.
```

We're nearly done, we'll just add an `ExampleController` so we have something to play with; Example 4-15 shows how to create a subclassed controller.

Example 4-15. controllers/example_controller.rb

```
class ExampleController < ApplicationController
  get '/' do
    title "Example Page"
    erb :example
  end
end
```

And we should create a corresponding view, shown in Example 4-16.

Example 4-16. controllers/example_controller.rb

```
<h1>This is an example page!</h1>
```

Now the real question is how to run it. We should go for using a *config.ru*, since the Rack DSL offers a third method besides `use` and `run`: `map`. This nifty method allows you to map a given path to a Rack endpoint. We can use that to serve multiple Sinatra apps from the same process; Example 4-17 shows how to do so.

Example 4-17. config.ru

```
require 'sinatra/base'
Dir.glob('./{helpers,controllers}/*.rb').each { |file| require file }

map('/example') { run ExampleController }
map('/') { run ApplicationController }
```

Rack will remove the path supplied to `map` from the request path and store it safely in `env['SCRIPT_NAME']`. Sinatra's `url` helper will pick it up to construct correct links for you.

Dynamic Subclass Generation

Sometimes you might want to generate new Sinatra applications on the fly without having to create a new constant. A typical example is testing your application or Sinatra extension, but there are lots of other use cases. You can simply use `Sinatra.new` to create an anonymous, modular application as shown in Example 4-18.

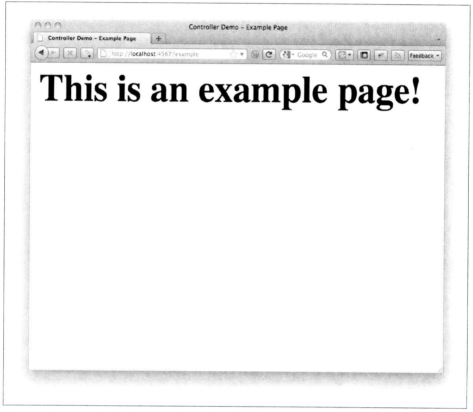

Figure 4-4. map makes the ExampleController available

Example 4-18. Using Sinatra.new in a config.ru

```
require 'sinatra/base'

app = Sinatra.new do
  get('/') { 'Hello World!' }
end

run app
```

Just like when creating constants, you may choose to use a different superclass to inherit from. Simply pass that class in as argument.

Example 4-19. Using a different superclass

```
require 'sinatra/base'

general_app = Sinatra.new { enable :logging }
custom_app = Sinatra.new(general_app) do
  get('/') { 'Hello World!' }
end
```

```
run custom_app
```

You can use this to dynamically generate new Sinatra applications.

Example 4-20. Dynamically generating Sinatra applications

```
require 'sinatra/base'

words = %w[foo bar blah]

words.each do |word|
  # generate a new application for each word
  map "/#{word}" { run Sinatra.new { get('/') { word } } }
end

map '/' do
  app = Sinatra.new do
    get '/' do
      list = words.map do |word|
        "<a href='/#{word}'>#{word}</a>"
      end
      list.join("<br>")
    end
  end

  run app
end
```

Better Rack Citizenship

In a typical scenario for modular applications, you usually embrace the usage of Rack: setting up different endpoints, creating your own middleware, and so on. If you want to use Sinatra in there as much as possible, you will have a hard time trying to only use a classic style application. If you decide to not only use Rack to communicate to the web server, but also internally to achieve a modular and flexible architecture, Sinatra will try to help you wherever possible.

In return it will give you interoperability and open up a variety of already existing libraries and middleware, just waiting for you to use them.

Chaining Classes

We already talked about using map to serve more than one Sinatra application from the same Rack handler. But this is not the only way to combine multiple apps.

Middleware Chain

If you followed along in Chapter 3 closely, you might have arrived at this next point intuitively. We demonstrated how to use a Sinatra application as middleware. You are certainly free to use one Sinatra application as middleware in front of another Sinatra application. This will first try to find a route in the middleware application, and if that middleware application does not find a matching route, it will hand the request on to the other application, as shown in Example 4-21.

Example 4-21. Using Sinatra as endpoint and middleware

```
require 'sinatra/base'

class Foo < Sinatra::Base
  get('/foo') { 'foo' }
end

class Bar < Sinatra::Base
  get('/bar') { 'bar' }

  use Foo
  run!
end
```

This allows us to create a slightly different class architecture, where classes are not responsible for a specific set of paths, but instead may define any routes. If we combine this with Ruby's inherited hook for automatically tracking subclass creation (as in Example 4-22), we don't even have to keep a list of classes around.

Example 4-22. Automatically picking up subclasses as middleware

```
require 'sinatra/base'

class ApplicationController < Sinatra::Base
  def self.inherited(sublass)
    super
    use sublass
  end

  enable :logging
end

class ExampleController < Sinatra::Base
  get('/example') { "Example!" }
end

# works with dynamically generated applications, too
Sinatra.new ApplicationController do
  get '/' do
    "See the <a href='/example'>example</a>."
  end
end

ApplicationController.run!
```

If you define `inherited` on a Ruby class, always make sure you call `super`. Sinatra uses `inherited`, too, in order to set up a new application class properly. If you skip the `super` call, the class will not be set up properly.

Cascade

There is an alternative that seems rather similar at first glance: using a cascade rather than a middleware chain. It works pretty much the same. You supply a list of Rack application, which will be tried one after the other, and the first result that doesn't have a status code of 404 will be returned. For a basic demonstration, Example 4-23 will behave exactly like a middleware chain.

Example 4-23. Using Rack::Cascade with rackup

```
require 'sinatra/base'

class Foo < Sinatra::Base
  get('/foo') { 'foo' }
end

class Bar < Sinatra::Base
  get('/bar') { 'bar' }
end

run Rack::Cascade, [Foo, Bar]
```

There are a few minor differences to using middleware. First of all, the behavior of passing on the request if no route matches is Sinatra specific. With a cascade, you can use any endpoints; you might first try a Rails application and a Sinatra application after that. Moreover, imagine you explicitly return a 404 error from a Sinatra application, for instance with `get('/') { not_found }`. If you do that in a middleware and the route matches, the request will never be handed on to the second application; with a cascade, it will be. See Example 4-24 for a concrete implementation of this concept.

Example 4-24. Handing on a request with not_found

```
require 'sinatra/base'

class Foo1 < Sinatra::Base
  get('/foo') { not_found }
end

class Foo2 < Sinatra::Base
  get('/foo') { 'foo #2' }
end

run Rack::Cascade, [Foo1, Foo2]
```

If you happen to have a larger number of endpoints, using a cascade is likely to result in better performance, at least on the official Ruby implementation.

Ruby uses a *Mark-And-Sweep Garbage Collector* to remove objects from memory that are no longer needed (usually it's just called the *GC*), which will walk through all stack frames to mark objects that are not supposed to be removed. Since a middleware chain is a recursive structure, each middleware will add at least one stack frame, increasing the amount of work the GC has to deal with.

Since Ruby's GC also is a *Stop-The-World GC*, your Ruby process will not be able to do anything else while it is collecting garbage.

With a Router

A third option is using a Rack *router*. We've already used the most simple router a few times: `Rack::URLMap`. It ships with the `rack` gem and is used by Rack under the hood for its `map` method. However, there are a lot more routers out there for Rack with different capabilities and characteristics. In a way, Sinatra is a router, too, or at least can be used as such, but more on that later.

A router is similar to a Rack middleware. The main difference is that it doesn't wrap a single Rack endpoint, but keeps a list of endpoints, just like `Rack::Cascade` does. Depending on some criteria, usually the requested path, the router will then decide what endpoint to hand the request to. This is basically the same thing Sinatra does, except that it doesn't hand off the request. Instead, it decides what block of code to evaluate.

Most routers differ in the way they decide which endpoint to hand the request to. All routers meant for general usage do offer routing based on the path, but how complex their path matching might be varies. While `Rack::URLMap` only matches prefixes, most other routers allow simple wildcard matching. Both `Rack::Mount`, which is used by Rails, and Sinatra allow arbitrary matching logic.

However, such flexibility comes at a price: `Rack::Mount` and Sinatra have a routing complexity of $O(n)$, meaning that in the worst-case scenario an incoming request has to be matched against all the defined routes. Usually this doesn't matter much, though. We did some experiments replacing the Sinatra routing logic with a less capable version, that does routing in $O(1)$, and we didn't see any performance benefits for applications with fewer than about *10,000* routes.

`Rack::Mount` is known to produce fast routing, however its API is not meant to be used directly but rather by other libraries, like the Rails routes DSL. Install it by running **gem install rack-mount**. Example 4-25 demonstrates how to use it.

Example 4-25. Using Rack::Mount in a config.ru

```
require 'sinatra/base'
require 'rack/mount'
```

```
class Foo < Sinatra::Base
  get('/foo') { 'foo' }
end

class Bar < Sinatra::Base
  get('/bar') { 'bar' }
end

Routes = Rack::Mount::RouteSet.new do |set|
  set.add_route Foo, :path_info => %r{^/foo$}
  set.add_route Bar, :path_info => %r{^/bar$}
end

run Routes
```

It also supports other criteria besides the path. For instance, you can easily send different HTTP methods to different endpoints, as in Example 4-26.

Example 4-26. Route depending on the verb

```
require 'sinatra/base'
require 'rack/mount'

class Get < Sinatra::Base
  get('/') { 'GET!' }
end

class Post < Sinatra::Base
  post('/') { 'POST!' }
end

Routes = Rack::Mount::RouteSet.new do |set|
  set.add_route Get,  :request_method => 'GET'
  set.add_route Post, :request_method => 'POST'
end

run Routes
```

On Return Values

The application's return value is an integral part of the Rack specification. Rack is picky on what you may return. Sinatra, on the other hand, is forgiving when it comes to return values. Sinatra routes commonly have a string value returned on the last line of the block, but it can also be any value conforming to the Rack specification. Example 4-27 demonstrates this.

Example 4-27. Running a Rack application with Sinatra

```
require 'sinatra'

# this is a valid Rack program
MyApp = proc { [200, {'Content-Type' => 'text/plain'}, ['ok']] }
```

```
# that you can run with Sinatra
get('/', &MyApp)
```

Besides strings and Rack arrays, it accepts a wide range of return values that look nearly like Rack return values. As the body object can be a string, you don't have to wrap it in an array. You don't have to include a headers hash either. Example 4-28 clarifies this point.

Example 4-28. Alternative return values

```
require 'sinatra'

get('/') { [418, "I'm a tea pot!"] }
```

You can also push a return value through the wire any time using the halt helper, like in Example 4-29.

Example 4-29. Alternative return values

```
require 'sinatra'

get '/' do
  halt [418, "I'm a tea pot!"]
  "You'll never get here!"
end
```

With halt you can pass the array elements as separate arguments. This helper is especially useful in filters (as in Example 4-30), where you can use it to directly send the response.

Example 4-30. Alternative return values

```
require 'sinatra'

before { halt 418, "I'm a tea pot!" }
get('/') { "You'll never get here!" }
```

Using Sinatra as Router

Since Sinatra accepts Rack return values, you can use the return value of another Rack endpoint, as shown in Example 4-31. Remember: all Rack applications respond to call, which takes the env hash as argument.

Example 4-31. Using another Rack endpoint in a route

```
require 'sinatra/base'

class Foo < Sinatra::Base
  get('/') { "Hello from Foo!" }
end

class Bar < Sinatra::Base
```

```
  get('/') { Foo.call(env) }
end

Bar.run!
```

We can easily use this to implement a Rack router. Let's implement `Rack::Mount` from Example 4-31 with Sinatra instead, as shown in Example 4-32.

Example 4-32. Using Sinatra as router

```
require 'sinatra/base'

class Foo < Sinatra::Base
  get('/foo') { 'foo' }
end

class Bar < Sinatra::Base
  get('/bar') { 'bar' }
end

class Routes < Sinatra::Base
  get('/foo') { Foo.call(env) }
  get('/bar') { Bar.call(env) }
end

run Routes
```

And of course, we can also implement the method-based routing easily, as shown in Example 4-33.

Example 4-33. Verb based routing with Sinatra

```
require 'sinatra/base'

class Get < Sinatra::Base
  get('/') { 'GET!' }
end

class Post < Sinatra::Base
  post('/') { 'POST!' }
end

class Routes < Sinatra::Base
  get('/') { Get.call(env) }
  post('/') { Post.call(env) }
end

run Routes
```

Extensions and Modular Applications

Let's recall the two common ways to extend Sinatra applications: extensions and help-ers. Both are usable just the way they are in classic applications. However, let's take a closer look at them again.

Helpers

Helpers are instance methods and therefore available both in route blocks and views. We can still use the `helpers` method to import methods from a module or to pass a block with methods to it, just the way we did in Chapter 3. See Example 4-34.

Example 4-34. Using helpers in a modular application

```ruby
require 'sinatra/base'
require 'date'

module MyHelpers
  def time
    Time.now.to_s
  end
end

class MyApplication < Sinatra::Base
  helpers MyApplication

  helpers do
    def date
      Date.today.to_s
    end
  end

  get('/') { "it's #{time}\n" }
  get('/today') { "today is #{date}\n" }

  run!
end
```

However, in the end, those methods will become normal instance methods, so there is actually no need to define them specially. See Example 4-35.

Example 4-35. Helpers are just instance methods

```ruby
require 'sinatra/base'

class MyApplication < Sinatra::Base
  def time
    Time.now.to_s
  end

  get('/') { "it's #{time}\n" }
```

```
    run!
end
```

Extensions

Extensions generally add DSL methods used at load time, just like get, before, and so on. Just like helpers, those can be defined on the class directly. See Example 4-36 for a demonstration of using class methods.

Example 4-36. Using class methods

```
require 'sinatra/base'

class MyApplication < Sinatra::Base
  def self.get_and_post(*args, &block)
    get(*args, &block)
    post(*args, &block)
  end

  get_and_post '/' do
    "Thanks for your #{request.request_method} request."
  end

  run!
end
```

Previously, we introduced a common pattern for reusable extensions: you call Sina tra.register Extension in the file defining the extension, you just have to require that file, and it will work automatically. This is only true for classic applications, we still have to register the extension explicitly in modular applications, as seen in Example 4-37.

Example 4-37. Extensions and modular applications

```
require 'sinatra/base'
module Sinatra
  module GetAndPost
    def get_and_post(*args, &block)
      get(*args, &block)
      post(*args, &block)
    end
  end

  # this will only affect Sinatra::Application
  register GetAndPost
end

class MyApplication < Sinatra::Base
  register Sinatra::GetAndPost

  get_and_post '/' do
    "Thanks for your #{request.request_method} request."
  end
```

```
  run!
end
```

Why this overhead? Automatically registering extensions for modular applications is not as appealing as it might appear at first glance. Modular applications usually travel in packs: if one application loads an extension, you don't want to drag that extension into other application classes by accident.

Summary

We introduced modular applications in this chapter, which allows us to easily build more complex and flexible architectures. We discussed how to run and combine such applications and while doing so, learned a few more things about Rack.

## CHAPTER 5

Hands On: Your Own Blog Engine

Like so many others, most open source developers run their own public blog. But there is a huge difference between open source developers and other people: while most "normal" people have to decide what kind of blogging software to use, developers tend to decide what kind of blogging software to implement. The reason for this? A blogging software is actually extremely simple to implement if you just want to have a single, simple workflow for blogging. This makes custom blogging software (the *blog engine*) way more appealing. And doesn't it seem like a small and fun project?

Let's build on what we've learned in the recent chapters about modular applications and Rack to build our own little blog engine.

Workflow Concept

As programmers, we can get quite passionate about what text editor or IDE to use for writing code. Why should we be less opinionated when it comes to writing blog posts? In-browser editors have become quite impressive as of late. But embedding those in a blog engine just for getting syntax highlighting? Instead, let's avoid dealing with authorization and the security issues involved with implementing an in-browser editor and having to set it up properly by simply not doing it at all.

What if we could use our favorite editor to write blog posts and use git to keep track of versioning? This would, among other things, give us all the features Git comes with: tracking changes made to the posts, creating different branches for working on not-yet-released posts, even easing collaboration for blogs written by more than one author.

File-Based Posts

For simplicity, let's store articles in the same repository we store our blog engine in. It should be fairly easy for you to separate it into two repositories, in case you favor that approach. To keep things organized, we'll store those articles in the *articles* folder and the Ruby code in *lib*.

We'll use the popular *Markdown* markup language for formatting the blog posts. It will also allow you to embed arbitrary HTML in your articles, which comes in handy if you want to embed media like a YouTube movie.

> Since we will rely on Sinatra for translating our Markdown articles into HTML, you can easily choose any other template language supported by Sinatra, like *Textile*. You can learn more about Markdown at *http://daringfireball.net/projects/markdown/*.

Like most other text-based blog engines, let's store the posts metadata in YAML format at the beginning of the article. We should probably stick to the minimum of data for this exercise, but what we do need is the date the article was published and the title. A simple blog post is shown in Example 5-1.

> If you feel like experimenting even further, try removing all metadata from the files and parse title and date from the generated HTML and git logs respectively once you have your blog running.

Example 5-1. A typical blog post: articles/updated.md

```
title: Updated
date: 2011-09-25

Hello friends! Sorry, I haven't blogged in quite a while. I was busy reading
[a book](http://oreilly.com/catalog/0636920019664/) to improve my Sinatra
skills. I will blog more from now on, I promise.
```

Git for Distribution

We still want the workflow to be as simple as possible. In an ideal scenario we could simply **git push** to our blog in order to update it, similar to how you would deploy on Heroku. And since it would be cool to avoid a vendor lock-in, let's try to implement that feature on our own, without having to host our application on Heroku.

> If you are new to Git, you can learn more about it at *http://git-scm .com/*. It is essentially a distributed, patch based *Version Control System*.
>
> For this tutorial it is important to know that Git commits are explicitly pushed to a remote repository and are identified by a *commit hash*.

Ideally, we want to be able to push our updates to GitHub and that's it. That would also allow us to use the embedded web editor GitHub offers, shown in Figure 5-1, in case we run into a situation where we don't have Git installed locally or don't want to

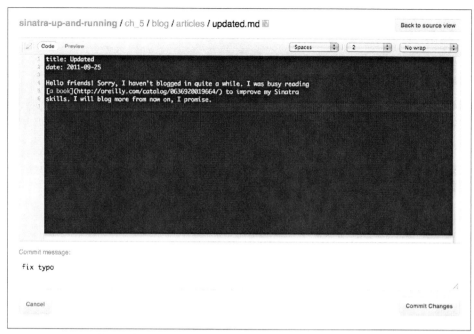

sinatra-up-and-running / ch_5 / blog / articles / **updated.md**

Back to source view

| Code | Preview | Spaces | 2 | No wrap |

```
title: Updated
date: 2011-09-25

Hello friends! Sorry, I haven't blogged in quite a while. I was busy reading
[a book](http://oreilly.com/catalog/0636920019664/) to improve my Sinatra
skills. I will blog more from now on, I promise.
```

Commit message:

fix typo

Cancel

Commit Changes

Figure 5-1. Being able to edit posts on GitHub

clone the repository just for editing a blog post. We will look into how to implement this without writing any code that is GitHub specific, again to avoid a vendor lock-in.

 We use GitHub as an example here, as it is rather popular among Ruby developers and you will find almost all Ruby related projects there. You could of course use any alternative platform. Popular ones include *Bit bucket* and *Gitorious*.

Semistatic Pages

Apart from updating or adding an article, a blog is actually a rather static website. While it seems a bit boring at first, we can easily use that to our advantage. An important goal for most websites out there is to serve as many requests per second as possible in the most efficient way. While it is probably true that developer time is more expensive than server time, it seems rather unreasonable to serve a simple blog from more than one machine. Even serving it from more than one process on that machine seems unreasonable in most cases.

Since articles will not change unless we push an update upstream, there is no reason to read them from disk more often than that. The general idea is to spend as little time as possible in the Ruby process when a request comes in. We will look into how to reduce that time even further and how to keep requests from reaching the Ruby process in the first place by setting the proper HTTP headers.

The Implementation

Reloading the application on changes and actually displaying the articles are two separate concerns not tightly coupled to each other. As software developers we have learned to reflect such separations in the code to keep it clean and flexible. So, why not create two separate Sinatra applications for those tasks? It seems reasonable to serve the posts from a Rack endpoint. Now we could set up the update logic as another endpoint, but for such a simple app it's easier to create a middleware for it.

Displaying Blog Posts

First we need to create a modular application for serving the articles, as shown in Example 5-2. Since we don't want to store views and static assets like stylesheets and images inside *lib*, we have to make sure that we set the root property properly.

Example 5-2. Setting up a modular application (lib/blog.rb)

```
require 'sinatra/base'

class Blog < Sinatra::Base
  # File.expand_path generates an absolute path.
  # It also takes a path as second argument. The
  # generated path is treated as being relative
  # to that path.
  set :root, File.expand_path('../../', __FILE__)
end
```

Rendering Markdown

Sinatra supports quite a large number of rendering engines. We already used the erb method for rendering ERB templates. Sinatra offers a similar method called markdown for - surprise, surprise - Markdown templates. As we've seen before, we can pass symbols to those methods to render files from the *views* directory. But you don't always have the source stored in a view file. That's why you can pass a string to those methods instead and Sinatra will treat that string as the template source code. See Example 5-3.

Example 5-3. Rendering Markdown from a string

```
get('/') { markdown "# A Headline" }
```

Since these rendering methods simply return strings, you can easily embed the result in another template, as seen in Example 5-4.

Example 5-4. Embedding Markdown in ERB

```
<h1>Markdown in ERB</h1>
<%= markdown("This is *Markdown*!") %>
```

 While ERB ships with Ruby, there is no Markdown implementation in the standard library. Sinatra will automatically pick up any implementation you have installed on your system. However, if you have none, you need to install one: **gem install rdiscount**.

Generating articles

Since we do not care about Git updates in the blog logic, let's load all the articles when loading the application. See Example 5-5.

Example 5-5. Loading articles (lib/blog.rb)

```
require 'sinatra/base'
require 'ostruct'
require 'time'

class Blog < Sinatra::Base
  set :root, File.expand_path('../../', __FILE__)

  # loop through all the article files
  Dir.glob "#{root}/articles/*.md" do |file|
    # parse meta data and content from file
    meta, content   = File.read(file).split("\n\n", 2)

    # generate a metadata object
    article         = OpenStruct.new YAML.load(meta)

    # convert the date to a time object
    article.date    = Time.parse article.date.to_s

    # add the content
    article.content = content

    # generate a slug for the url
    article.slug    = File.basename(file, '.md')

    # set up the route
    get "/#{article.slug}" do
      erb :post, :locals => { :article => article }
    end
  end
end
```

 We are using the *ostruct* library that comes with Ruby. It is a small wrapper around hashes, exposing setters and getters for all the hash entries.

We still need a view for rendering these articles, shown in Example 5-6. We'll use HTML5 tags, since we like to use all the fancy new technology out there to keep up with recent development.

Example 5-6. views/post.erb

```
<article>
  <header>
    <h1>
      <a href="<%= url(article.slug) %>"><%= article.title %></a>
    </h1>
    <time class="timeago" datetime="<%= article.date.xmlschema %>">
      <%= article.date.strftime "%Y/%m/%d" %>
    </time>
  </header>
  <section class="content">
    <%= markdown article.content %>
  </section>
</article>
```

Adding an index

We also want a home page displaying all the articles. Since we keep the articles in-process, there is no reason not to do the same for the list of articles; Example 5-7 shows the Sinatra wiring necessary for this, and Example 5-8 provides an Erb template for rendering.

Example 5-7. Loading articles (lib/blog.rb)

```
require 'sinatra/base'
require 'ostruct'
require 'time'

class Blog < Sinatra::Base
  set :root, File.expand_path('../../', __FILE__)
  set :articles, []

  Dir.glob "#{root}/articles/*.md" do |file|
    meta, content    = File.read(file).split("\n\n", 2)
    article          = OpenStruct.new YAML.load(meta)
    article.date     = Time.parse article.date.to_s
    article.content = content
    article.slug     = File.basename(file, '.md')

    get "/#{article.slug}" do
      erb :post, :locals => { :article => article }
    end

    # Add article to list of articles
    articles << article
  end

  # Sort articles by date, display new articles first
  articles.sort_by! { |article| article.date }
```

```
  articles.reverse!

  get '/' do
    erb :index
  end
end
```

Example 5-8. views/index.erb

```
<% settings.articles.each do |article| %>
  <%= erb :post, :locals => { :article => article } %>
<% end %>
```

Adding a basic layout

The pages we're generating at the moment are more or less incomplete HTML documents. A simple layout file fixes this. See Example 5-9.

Example 5-9. views/layout.erb

```
<!DOCTYPE html>
<html>
  <head>
    <title>My Blog</title>
    <link rel="stylesheet" media="screen" href="/css/blog.css" />
    <script type="text/javascript" src="/js/jquery.min.js"></script>
    <script type="text/javascript" src="/js/jquery.timeago.js"></script>
    <script type="text/javascript" src="/js/blog.js"></script>
  </head>
  <body>
    <%= yield %>
  </body>
</html>
```

As you can see in Example 5-10, we added the *timeago* JQuery plug-in to automatically format our date strings. You can learn more about that plugin at *http://timeago.yarp .com/*.

Example 5-10. public/js/blog.js

```
$(document).ready(function() {
  $("time.timeago").timeago();
});
```

And to have a nicer first impression, let's add some CSS right away. This will also give you a nice starting point to adding a better layout later on. See Example 5-11 for CSS and Figure 5-2 for a first look at the blog.

Example 5-11. public/css/blog.css

```
body {
  font-family: "Helvetica Neue", Arial, Helvetica, sans-serif;
}
```

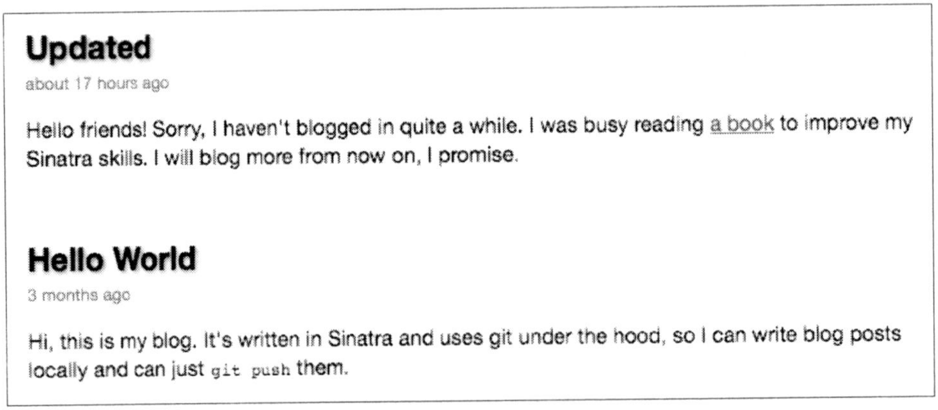

Figure 5-2. A first look at the blog

```
article {
  min-width: 300px;
  max-width: 700px;
  margin: 50px auto;
  padding: 0 50px;
}

header h1 {
  margin: 0;
}

header a {
  color: #000;
  text-decoration: none;
  text-shadow: 1px 1px 2px #555;
}

header a:hover {
  text-decoration: underline;
}

header time {
  font-size: 80%;
  color: #555;
}
```

Git Integration

As mentioned before, the goal is to automatically update the blog whenever pushing to the blog repository. Most hosting sites, like GitHub or Bitbucket, offer service hooks: they will trigger a request to a custom URL whenever someone pushes new commits to the repository. Even if you host the repository on your own server, you can easily set up a so-called post-receive hook there. But let's first look into the implementation before we go into setting everything up.

Regenerating content

To regenerate the content, all we have to do is reload our application. We could do that by restarting the process. However, that might be complicated to implement and cause our website to be down for a moment.

Another idea would be to simply load *lib/blog.rb* again. However, that would append the routes to the list of already defined routes rather than overriding existing routes. That approach works for adding new posts, but would prohibit editing existing posts. Moreover, it would leak memory, since old routes would never be removed.

We need to remove all the routes before loading the file again. But it doesn't stop there, we also need to get rid of all the filters, middleware, error handlers, and so on. We are not using all those features at the moment, but we don't want to break our app later on if we add a middleware or error handler. Luckily Sinatra has a mechanism for doing exactly that: the reset! method.

Let's assume that in the middleware we're creating, the wrapped endpoint (stored in app) is the Sinatra class we want to wrap. In that case we have reset! and the file that we want to reload available. The file is stored in the app_file setting. Sinatra takes care of setting it to the correct value. Example 5-12 demonstrates how to do this.

Example 5-12. Regenerating content (lib/github_hook.rb)

```
require 'sinatra/base'
require 'time'

class GithubHook < Sinatra::Base
  post '/update' do
    app.settings.reset!
    load app.settings.app_file

    content_type :txt
    "ok"
  end
end
```

The above middleware will reload our application whenever /update is being requested. We can use that when setting up a hook later on.

Pulling changes

When running on the server, we also want to automatically trigger a **git pull** to fetch the commits we just pushed from our local development machine to our source code repository and deploy them on our productions server. However, we probably don't want to trigger a pull while in development. That way we can easily trigger a reload while working on a post without causing trouble with Git trying to pull in changes, as seen in Example 5-13.

Let's introduce a setting called :autopull that specifies whether or not to trigger a pull on a reload and make that setting dependent on the current environment.

Example 5-13. Pulling changes (lib/github_hook.rb)

```ruby
require 'sinatra/base'
require 'time'

class GithubHook < Sinatra::Base
  set(:autopull) { production? }

  post '/update' do
    app.settings.reset!
    load app.settings.app_file

    content_type :txt
    if settings.autopull?
      # Pipe stderr to stdout to make
      # sure we display everything.
      `git pull 2>&1`
    else
      "ok"
    end
  end
end
```

Proper cache headers

We want our page to render as quickly as possible and at the same time keep the load on our server as low as we can. Fortunately HTTP comes with a handful of headers to aid us here. We covered the basics of HTTP caching in Chapter 2, let's see how best to utilize them.

First of all, we want to avoid outdated caches at any cost. We also want to allow public caching, since our blog is public. We'll therefore call `cache_control :public, :must_revalidate`. To allow revalidation, we need to set at least either an `ETag` or a `Last-Modified` header. Let's do both.

Since our blog is git-based, we can simply ask Git when the content has last been modified, and we can use the *Commit Hash* as `ETag`. And since we know when new commits are coming in, we only have to ask Git for the information whenever the update hook is triggered. Example 5-14 demonstrates how to probe Git for update information.

Example 5-14. lib/github_hook.rb

```ruby
require 'sinatra/base'
require 'time'

class GithubHook < Sinatra::Base
  def self.parse_git
    # Parse hash and date from the git log command.
    sha1, date = `git log HEAD~1..HEAD --pretty=format:%h^%ci`.strip.split('^')
    set :commit_hash, sha1
    set :commit_date, Time.parse(date)
  end
```

```
    set(:autopull) { production? }
    parse_git

    before do
      cache_control :public, :must_revalidate
      etag settings.commit_hash
      last_modified settings.commit_date
    end

    post '/update' do
      settings.parse_git

      app.settings.reset!
      load app.settings.app_file

      content_type :txt
      if settings.autopull?
        `git pull 2>&1`
      else
        "ok"
      end
    end
  end
end
```

Glueing Everything Together

What we still need to do is actually set up the GithubHook middleware in our Blog application. As with all middleware, we do that with the use method in Example 5-15.

Example 5-15. lib/blog.rb

```
require 'sinatra/base'
require 'github_hook'
require 'ostruct'
require 'time'

class Blog < Sinatra::Base
  use GithubHook

  set :root, File.expand_path('../../', __FILE__)
  set :articles, []
  set :app_file, __FILE__

  Dir.glob "#{root}/articles/*.md" do |file|
    meta, content  = File.read(file).split("\n\n", 2)
    article        = OpenStruct.new YAML.load(meta)
    article.date    = Time.parse article.date.to_s
    article.content = content
    article.slug    = File.basename(file, '.md')

    get "/#{article.slug}" do
      erb :post, :locals => { :article => article }
    end
```

```
    articles << article
  end

  articles.sort_by! { |article| article.date }
  articles.reverse!

  get '/' do
    erb :index
  end
end
```

Rack It Up!

For deployment we'll write a *config.ru*, as described earlier. To show a use case of the caching headers, let's add the `Rack::Cache` library (as shown in Example 5-16), which implements an HTTP cache as a Rack middleware. This is, of course, completely optional.

Example 5-16. config.ru

```
$LOAD_PATH.unshift 'lib'

# this is optional
require 'rack/cache'
use Rack::Cache

require 'blog'
run Blog
```

As discussed in Chapter 3, you can now start the server with the **rackup** command. When deploying on your production system, make sure you set the environment to production. Optionally, you can start **rackup** as a daemon, so it will run in the background: **rackup -E production -D -s thin**.

Setting it up on GitHub

Now that we're done with implementing our blog, let's publish it on GitHub. Log in with your GitHub account. On the Dashboard, click on *New Repository* and follow the instructions.

Once you have your repository set up, go to its *Admin* section, navigate to *Service Hooks*, and add a *Post-Receive URL* pointing to the */update* endpoint of your blog. See Figure 5-3.

Setting it up on Bitbucket

Bitbucket used to be a hosting site for *Mercurial* only, but it recently added support for Git. In contrast to GitHub, Bitbucket offers an unlimited number of private repositories for free. So, if you don't want anyone to see the code of your little blog engine, Bitbucket might be an interesting alternative.

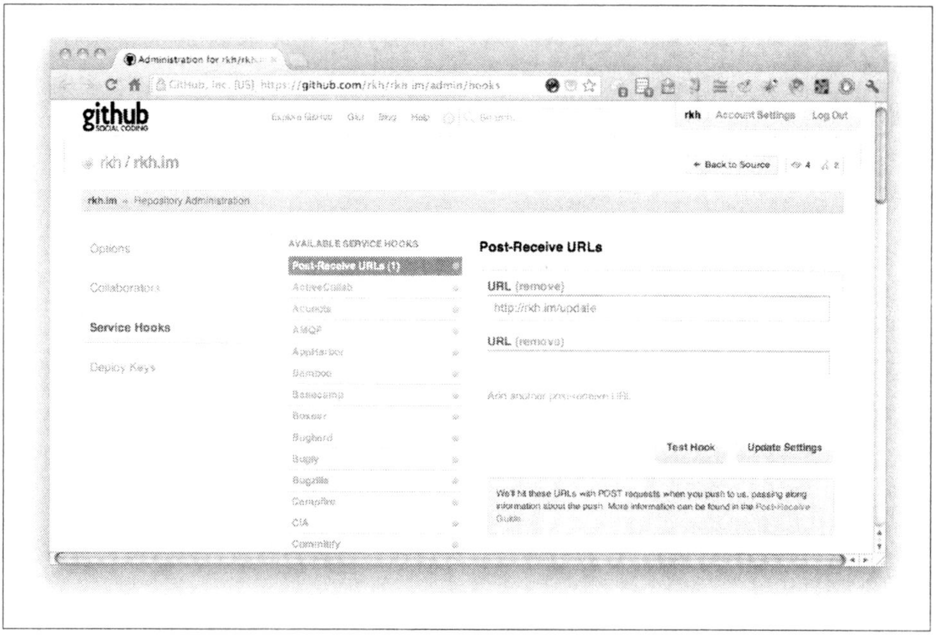

Figure 5-3. Setting up a service hook on GitHub

After logging in with your account, you can create a new repository by clicking the *create repository* link from the *Repositories* pop-up menu. Make sure you choose Git as *Repository type*. Again, just follow the instructions displayed after creating the repository.

Once you have your repository set up, go to its *Admin* section, navigate to *Services*, and add a *POST URL* pointing to the /update end-point of your blog. See Figure 5-4.

Using a post-receive hook

If you already are an experienced Git user, you might be tempted to set up your own repository somewhere. To set up a post-receive hook with your own repository, navigate to your repository on your server, create a file called *.git/hooks/post-receive* (see Example 5-17), and make that file executable, for instance by running **chmod +x .git/hooks/post-receive** on a Unix system. In this file we can add the logic for triggering such an update. Interestingly if you add a magic comment called *shebang* or *hashbang*, you can easily write that hook in Ruby.

Example 5-17. .git/hooks/post-receive

```
#!/usr/bin/env ruby
require 'open-uri'

# place your own URL here
open('http://localhost:4567/update')
```

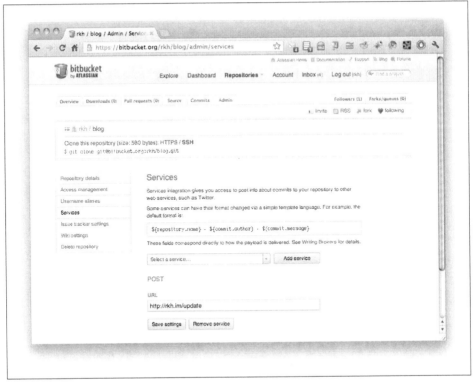

Figure 5-4. Setting up a service hook on Bitbucket

What about Heroku?

You might want to deploy your application on Heroku. Heroku has a read-only file-system, therefore you cannot have the blog automatically pull changes. Instead you have to push to Heroku explicitly. But it would be nice if we didn't have to throw away all of the GithubHook middleware. Since the only real issue is not being able to pull in changes, we can solve this situation by disabling the autopull setting we introduced earlier. And since Heroku comes with an HTTP cache, there is no need for setting up Rack::Cache.

Heroku sets a few environment variables to avoid any additional configuration, therefore the variables URL and DATABASE_URL are indicators for running on Heroku.

This configuration is not really part of the application logic. The best place to store it is probably in the *config.ru*, which you can see in Example 5-18.

Example 5-18. config.ru

```
$LOAD_PATH.unshift 'lib'
require 'blog'
```

```
if ENV['URL'] and ENV['DATABASE_URL']
  # we're on heroku, no cache needed
  # also, it's a read-only file system
  GithubHook.disable :autopull
elsif Blog.production?
  require 'rack/cache'
  use Rack::Cache
end

run Blog
```

Summary

Hopefully you have a running blog by now. With this tutorial we demonstrated how to use some of the tools Sinatra has to offer and how to address real problems that come up when implementing a web application.

About the Authors

Alan Harris is a software engineer with a decade of professional experience, and author of several books on software development spanning multiple platforms and languages. He has delivered numerous scalable, elegant solutions for companies ranging from non-profits to military subcontractors; he has also been a featured contributor in the developerWorks community. He currently works and resides in the DC area.

Konstantin Haase, as a current maintainer of Sinatra, is an Open Source developer by heart. Ruby has become his language of choice since 2005. He actively participates in the Ruby community and regularly contributes to different widespread projects, like Rubinius and Rack. In 2010, he successfully took part in the Ruby Summer Of Code, working on Rails internals. Haase is currently studying IT Systems Engineering at the Hasso Plattner Institute in Potsdam, Germany, and works part time as a software engineer at finnlabs in Berlin.

Get even more for your money.

Join the O'Reilly Community, and register the O'Reilly books you own. It's free, and you'll get:

- $4.99 ebook upgrade offer
- 40% upgrade offer on O'Reilly print books
- Membership discounts on books and events
- Free lifetime updates to ebooks and videos
- Multiple ebook formats, DRM FREE
- Participation in the O'Reilly community
- Newsletters
- Account management
- 100% Satisfaction Guarantee

Signing up is easy:

1. **Go to: oreilly.com/go/register**
2. **Create an O'Reilly login.**
3. **Provide your address.**
4. **Register your books.**

Note: English-language books only

To order books online:
oreilly.com/store

For questions about products or an order:
orders@oreilly.com

To sign up to get topic-specific email announcements and/or news about upcoming books, conferences, special offers, and new technologies:
elists@oreilly.com

For technical questions about book content:
booktech@oreilly.com

To submit new book proposals to our editors:
proposals@oreilly.com

O'Reilly books are available in multiple DRM-free ebook formats. For more information:
oreilly.com/ebooks

O'REILLY®

Spreading the knowledge of innovators | oreilly.com

The information you need, when and where you need it.

With Safari Books Online, you can:

Access the contents of thousands of technology and business books

- Quickly search over 7000 books and certification guides
- Download whole books or chapters in PDF format, at no extra cost, to print or read on the go
- Copy and paste code
- Save up to 35% on O'Reilly print books
- **New!** Access mobile-friendly books directly from cell phones and mobile devices

Stay up-to-date on emerging topics before the books are published

- Get on-demand access to evolving manuscripts.
- Interact directly with authors of upcoming books

Explore thousands of hours of video on technology and design topics

- Learn from expert video tutorials
- Watch and replay recorded conference sessions

O'REILLY®

Spreading the knowledge of innovators   safari.oreilly.com